FOOD FOR THOUGHT

More anthologies available from
Macmillan Collector's Library

The Joy of Walking

The Art of Solitude

Why Friendship Matters

FOOD FOR THOUGHT

Selected Writings

Edited and introduced by
ANNIE GRAY

MACMILLAN COLLECTOR'S LIBRARY

This collection first published 2020 by Macmillan Collector's Library
an imprint of Pan Macmillan
The Smithson, 6 Briset Street, London ECIM 5NR
Associated companies throughout the world
www.panmacmillan.com

ISBN 978-1-5290-3261-1

1 3 5 7 9 8 6 4 2

A CIP catalogue record for this book is available from the British Library.

Casing design and endpaper pattern by Andrew Davidson
Typeset in Plantin by Jouve (UK), Milton Keynes
Printed and bound in China by Imago

Visit www.panmacmillan.com to read more about all our books
and to buy them. You will also find features, author interviews and
news of any author events, and you can sign up for e-newsletters
so that you're always first to hear about our new releases.

Contents

Introduction xi

PETRONIUS 1
'The Dinner of Trimalchio', from *The Satyricon*

ANON. 7
'Pancakes in the Manner of Tournai',
from *Le Ménagier de Paris*

ANON. 10
The Forme of Cury

BEN JONSON 12
'Inviting a Friend to Supper'

SAMUEL PEPYS 15
from *The Diary of Samuel Pepys*

ANON. 22
'The Women's Petition Against Coffee'

DANIEL DEFOE 28
from *Robinson Crusoe*

JONATHAN SWIFT 34
'Directions to the Cook',
from 'Directions to Servants'

WILLIAM VERRALL 45
'Preface', from *A Complete System of Cookery*

ELIZABETH RAFFALD 50
'Hen and Chickens in Jelly',
from *The Experienced English Housekeeper*

ROBERT BURNS 52
'Address to a Haggis'

JAMES BOSWELL 55
from Boswell's *Life of Samuel Johnson*

WILLIAM KITCHINER 59
from *The Cook's Oracle*

CHARLES LAMB 62
from *A Dissertation Upon Roast Pig*

WALTER SCOTT 67
from *Saint Ronan's Well*

CHRISTIAN ISOBEL JOHNSTONE
& WALTER SCOTT 75
from *The Cook and Housewife's Manual*

JEAN ANTHELME BRILLAT-SAVARIN 80
'Aphorisms of the Professor', from *The Physiology of Taste*

JEAN ANTHELME BRILLAT-SAVARIN 84
'Gastronomical Industry of the Émigrés',
from *The Physiology of Taste*

WILLIAM COBBETT 88
from *Rural Rides*

CHARLES GREVILLE 94
from *The Diary of Charles Greville*

WILLIAM THACKERAY 98
from *Memorials of Gourmandising*

CHARLES DICKENS 102
from *A Christmas Carol*

WILLIAM YARRELL 109
'To Roast a Swan', from *A History of British Birds*

HENRY MAYHEW 111
'Of the Street Sellers of Hot Eels and Pea-Soup',
from *London Labour and the London Poor*

ELIZA ACTON 121
from *The English Bread Book*

ALEXIS SOYER 126
from *Culinary Campaign*

OWEN MEREDITH 135
'Lucile'

CHARLES SELBY 138
'English Dinner for Snobs', from
The Dinner Question

ISABELLA BEETON 145
'Victoria Sandwiches', from *Book of Household Management*

MARY ELIZABETH BRADDON 147
from *Lady Audley's Secret*

LEWIS CARROLL 151
from *Alice in Wonderland*

HENRY LABOUCHÈRE 159
from *Diary of the Besieged Resident in Paris*

MARY ELIZABETH BRADDON 163
from *Hostages to Fortune*

ABBY FISHER 168
from *What Mrs. Fisher Knows About Old Southern Cooking*

AGNES MARSHALL 175
'Iced Spinach à la Crème', from *The Book of Ices*

FANNY LEMIRA GILLETTE & HUGO ZIEMANN 177
'Table Etiquette', from *The White House Cookbook*

MARY KROUT 181
from *A Looker-On in London*

ELIZABETH ROBBINS PENNELL 189
'The Simple Sole', from *Feasts of Autolycus*

ANON. 194
'She Cooked the Dinner'

GABRIEL TSCHUMI 196
from *Royal Chef*

GEORGE SIMS 203
'London's Light Refreshments',
from *Living London*

G. R. M. DEVEREUX 214
'The Orange', from *Etiquette for Men*

FRANK SCHLOESSER 217
from *The Cult of the Chafing Dish*

AGNES JEKYLL 222
'Meatless Meals', from *Kitchen Essays*

COUNTESS MORPHY 228
'Fricassée of Iguana', from *Recipes of All Nations*

FRANCIS LADRY 230
'Lord Woolton Pie'

GEORGE ORWELL 232
'In Defence of English Cooking'

NEVIL SHUTE 238
from *The Far Country*

Introduction
ANNIE GRAY

Food is one of the fundamentals of life. At a basic level, we would die without it. Eating is one of the few certainties of human existence, and occasions to eat are threaded into our lives, both on an everyday and a highly ritualized basis. Food is so embedded in our cultures and our psyches that it defines us: how we eat, what we eat, and our beliefs about what and how we eat are among our most talked about, worried over, and deeply held values.

This collection of food writing loosely covers the development of British and British-influenced food from around the discovery of the ingredients of the New World at the end of the Middle Ages to the near-death of British cuisine after fourteen years of rationing during the Second World War. It ranges from the parties of the super-rich to the desperation of the achingly poor, and from the bright lights and easy access to food shops of the city, to the vegetable plots and fields of the remote countryside. Some writers gently muse, others hector from above. There are recipes, both practical and fantastical, and the fruits of long experience of both cooking and dining. There are chefs and cooks, eaters and diners. Fiction jostles with poetry which sits next to angry ranting and opposite a quiet onlooker.

Think of it as a dinner party: some guests you like, some you admire, and some you aren't sure you want to see again, though it was fun at the time. The food, of course, is fabulous, the manners impeccable (to those who practise them, at least). You'll dip in and out of the conversation and, when it is all over, some of what you've experienced will stay with you. That, surely, is why it's all food for thought.

FOOD FOR THOUGHT

❦

PETRONIUS
27–66 AD

One of the most famous fictional dinner parties, the feast given by Gaius Pompeius Trimalchio, is a satire on excess. Written by Petronius, a Roman writer and nobleman in the time of Nero, only a fragment of *The Satyricon* survives. It tells the story of Encolpius, his friend and his slave lover, as they ricochet from orgies to fights.

Trimalchio, the dinner's host, is an ex-slave made good, a dissolute glutton married to an ex-dancer. His guests all talk too much (about sport, their own importance and the terrible decline in social manners), show off, insult their host as soon as his back is turned, and generally behave much like many bad dinner guests have for the last 2,000 years.

The conversation is dull, but the food is otherworldly. Prior to the boar stuffed with live thrushes served here, the diners have eaten honeyed dormice, pastry eggs stuffed with fig-peckers (a tiny warbler), and a zodiac-themed set of dishes including a pig's womb. Following it are at least another eight courses, ending with Trimalchio's mock-funeral and our narrator's rather queasy escape.

I

'The Dinner of Trimalchio', from *The Satyricon*

Trimalchio broke in upon this entertaining gossip, for the course had been removed and the guests, happy with wine, had started a general conversation: lying back upon his couch, "You ought to make this wine go down pleasantly," he said, "the fish must have something to swim in. But I say, you didn't think I'd be satisfied with any such dinner as you saw on the top of that tray? 'Is Ulysses no better known?' Well, well, we shouldn't forget our culture, even at dinner. May the bones of my patron rest in peace, he wanted me to become a man among men. No one can show me anything new, and that little tray has proved it. This heaven where the gods live, turns into as many different signs, and sometimes into the Ram: therefore, whoever is born under that sign will own many flocks and much wool, a hard head, a shameless brow, and a sharp horn. A great many school-teachers and rambunctious butters-in are born under that sign." We applauded the wonderful penetration of our astrologer and he ran on, "Then the whole heaven turns into a bull-calf and the kickers and herdsmen and those who see to it that their own bellies are full, come into the world.

Teams of horses and oxen are born under the Twins, and well-hung wenchers and those who bedung both sides of the wall. I was born under the Crab and therefore stand on many legs and own much property on land and sea, for the crab is as much at home on one as he is in the other. For that reason, I put nothing on that sign for fear of weighing down my own destiny. Bulldozers and gluttons are born under the Lion, and women and fugitives and chain-gangs are born under the Virgin. Butchers and perfumers are born under the Balance, and all who think that it is their business to straighten things out. Poisoners and assassins are born under the Scorpion. Cross-eyed people who look at the vegetables and sneak away with the bacon are born under the Archer. Horny-handed sons of toil are born under Capricorn. Bartenders and pumpkin-heads are born under the Water-Carrier. Caterers and rhetoricians are born under the Fishes: and so the world turns round, just like a mill, and something bad always comes to the top, and men are either being born or else they're dying. As to the sod and the honeycomb in the middle, for I never do anything without a reason, Mother Earth is in the centre, round as an egg, and all that is good is found in her, just like it is in a honeycomb."

3

"Bravo!" we yelled, and, with hands uplifted to the ceiling, we swore that such fellows as Hipparchus and Aratus were not to be compared with him. At length some slaves came in who spread upon the couches some coverlets upon which were embroidered nets and hunters stalking their game with boar-spears, and all the paraphernalia of the chase. We knew not what to look for next, until a hideous uproar commenced, just outside the dining-room door, and some Spartan hounds commenced to run around the table all of a sudden. A tray followed them, upon which was served a wild boar of immense size, wearing a liberty cap upon its head, and from its tusks hung two little baskets of woven palm fibre, one of which contained Syrian dates, the other, Theban. Around it hung little suckling pigs made from pastry, signifying that this was a brood-sow with her pigs at suck. It turned out that these were souvenirs intended to be taken home. When it came to carving the boar, our old friend Carver, who had carved the capons, did not appear, but in his place a great bearded giant, with bands around his legs, and wearing a short hunting cape in which a design was woven. Drawing his hunting-knife, he plunged it fiercely into the boar's side, and some thrushes flew out of the gash, fowlers, ready with their rods, caught them in a moment, as they fluttered around the room and Trimalchio ordered one to each guest, remarking, "Notice what fine acorns this forest-bred boar fed on," and as he spoke, some slaves removed the little baskets from the tusks and divided the Syrian and Theban dates equally among the diners.

Getting a moment to myself, in the meantime, I began to speculate as to why the boar had come with a liberty cap upon his head. After exhausting my invention with a thousand foolish guesses, I made bold to put the riddle which teased me to my old informant. "Why, sure," he replied, "even your slave could explain that; there's no riddle, everything's as plain as day! This boar made his first bow as the last course of yesterday's dinner and was dismissed by the guests, so today he comes back as a freedman!" I damned my stupidity and refrained from asking any more question for fear I might leave the impression that I had never dined among decent people before. While we were speaking, a handsome boy, crowned with vine leaves and ivy, passed grapes around, in a little basket, and impersonated Bacchus-happy, Bacchus-drunk, and Bacchus-dreaming, reciting, in the meantime, his master's verses, in a shrill voice.

Trimalchio turned to him and said, "Dionisus, be thou Liber," whereupon the boy immediately snatched the cap from the boar's head, and put it upon his own. At that Trimalchio added, "You can't deny that my father's middle name was Liber!" We applauded Trimalchio's conceit heartily, and kissed the boy as he went around. Trimalchio retired to the close-stool, after this course, and we, having freedom of action with the tyrant away, began to draw the other guests out. After calling for a bowl of wine, Dama spoke up, "A day's nothing at all: it's night before you can turn around, so you can't do better than to go right to the dining-room from your bed. It's been so cold that I can hardly get warm in a bath, but a hot drink's as good as an overcoat: I've had some long pegs, and between you and me, I'm a bit groggy; the booze has gone to my head."

ANON.

'Pancakes in the Manner of Tournai', from *Le Ménagier de Paris*, 1393

With the collapse of the Roman Empire, its ex-colonies lost much of their food knowledge. Over the next few hundred years new trade routes were established and, by the time of the first surviving culinary manuscripts, a new cuisine had developed, which could be just as elaborate as that of the Romans, but with different techniques and flavours. Many of the recipes written down in the fourteenth and fifteenth centuries are the antecedents of dishes we still cook today.

Le Ménagier de Paris purports to have been written by a wealthy Parisian for his young bride. It contains advice on a range of topics. The beauty is in the clarity of instruction, for example here, in clarifying the butter. It is rare for the presence of servants to be made obvious, but whoever is continually beating the paste, or should be wearied from mixing the batter, is not the gentle reader.

'Pancakes in the Manner of Tournai', from *Le Ménagier de Paris*

First: you should provide yourself with a copper or brass pan holding a quart, the mouth of which should be no wider than the bottom, or only very little, and the sides of which should be four or three and a half fingers high. *Item*: put in salted butter, melt it, skim it and clean it and then pour it into another pan, and leave all the salt behind. Add to it fresh fat as clean as can be. Then take eggs and fry them, and take the whites away from half of them and beat the remaining whites and all of the yolks, and then take a third or a quart of lukewarm white wine, and mix all of this together: then take the finest white wheaten flour that you can have, and beat everything together bit by bit, enough to tire out one or two people, and your paste should be neither thin nor thick, but such that it can gently run through a hole as big as a small finger; then put your butter and your fat on the fire together, as much of one as the other, until it boils, then take your paste and fill a bowl or big spoon of pierced wood and pour this into your fat, first in the middle of your pan, then turning it until the sides are filled; and keep beating your paste without ceasing so that you can make more crepes. And for each crepe that is in the pan you should lift it with a stick or skewer and turn it over to cook, then remove it, put it on a plate, and start another; and remember to always be moving and beating the remaining paste without stopping.

ANON.
The Forme of Cury

One of the earliest collections of recipes written in English, *The Forme of Cury* is a velum scroll containing recipes assembled by the cooks of Richard II. There are a number of versions, not all the same, and it was not published as a compendium until 1780.

The Forme of Cury roughly translates as 'method of cooking'. It contains recipes ranging from simple soups to salad dressing, along with courtly subtleties, which were highly complex and often largely ornamental showpieces. Familiar ingredients include olive oil, ginger and mace, along with the less familiar porpoise, hyssop and umbles (deer innards). This recipe, for blancmange, is based on rice pounded with chicken (capons), mixed with almond milk, sugar and spice (blaunche pouder was a prepared mixture of various spices, kept on hand as needed).

from *The Forme of Cury*

XIV. FOR TO MAKE BLOMANGER.

Nym rys and lefe hem and wafch hem clene and do thereto god almande mylk and feth hem tyl they al to breft and than lat hem kele and nym the lyre of the hennyn or of capoñs and grynd hem fmal keft therto wite grefe and boyle it. Nym blanchyd almandys and fafroñ and fet hem above in the dyfche and ferve yt forthe.

XXV. FOR TO MAKE MYLK ROFT.

Nym fwete mylk and do yt in a panne nym eyryn wyth al the wyte and fwyng hem wel and caft therto and colowre yt wyth fafroñ and boyl it tyl yt wexe thykke and thanne feth yt thorw a culdore and nym that levyth and preffe yt up on a bord and wan yt ys cold larde it and fcher yt on fchyverys and rofte yt on a grydern and ferve yt forthe.

BEN JONSON
1572–1637

One of the late Tudor era's best-known playwrights and poets, Ben Jonson had a colourful career including stints in the army, in prison, and as poet laureate. He wrote several of James I's court masques, often in collaboration with Inigo Jones (who designed the sets), setting the tone for a new dynasty as the Scottish Stuart monarchs sought to impose their personality on the court after the death of Elizabeth I.

Success at court depended on a strong network. William Herbert, Earl of Pembroke, was Jonson's most stalwart patron, and this collection, and indeed poem, was dedicated to him. The foods proposed are not those of the super-rich. Starting with palate-cleansing olives and continuing with meats with citrussy sauces, roast game, pastries and ending with cheese and fruit, Jonson's meal is muted. He even promises not to drink too much – possibly as Pooley and Parrot (government informers) have benefitted from his inebriation in the past.

'Inviting a Friend to Supper'

To Night, grave Sir, both my poor House, and I
     Do equally desire your Company:
Not that we think us worthy such a Guest,
     But that your worth will dignifie our Feast,
With those that come; whose Grace may make that seem
     Something, which, else, could hope for no esteem.
It is the fair Acceptance, Sir, creates
     The Entertainment perfect: not the Cates.
Yet shall you have, to rectifie your Palate,
     An Olive, Capers, or some better Sallad
Ush'ring the Mutton; with a short-leg'd Hen,
     If we can get her, full of Eggs, and then,
Limons, and Wine for Sauce: to these, a Coney
     Is not to be despair'd of, for our Money;
And, though Fowl, now, be scarce, yet there are Clarks,
     The Sky not falling, think we may have Larks.
I'll tell you of more, and lye, so you will come:
     Of Partridg, Pheasant, Wood-cock, of which some
May yet be there; and Godwit if we can:
     Knat, Rail, and Ruff too. How so ere, my Man
Shall read a Piece of *Virgil*, *Tacitus*,
     Livy, or of some better Book to us,
Of which we'll speak our Minds, amidst our Meat;
     And I'll profess no Verses to repeat:
To this, if ought appear, which I know not of,

That will the Pastry, not my Paper, show of.
Digestive Cheese, and Fruit there sure will be;

But that, which most doth take my *Muse*, and me,
Is a pure Cup of rich *Canary* Wine,

Which is the *Mermaids*, now, but shall be mine:
Of which had *Horace*, or *Anacreon* tasted,

Their Lives, as do their Lines, till now had lasted.
Tabacco, Nectar, or the *Thespian* Spring,

Are all but *Luther's* Beer, to this I sing.
Of this we will sup free, but moderately,

And we will have no *Pooly'*, or *Parrot* by;
Nor shall our Cups make any guilty Men:

But, at our parting, we will be, as when
We innocently met. No simple Word,

That shall be utter'd at our mirthful Board,
Shall make us sad next Morning: or affright

The Liberty, that we'll enjoy to Night.

SAMUEL PEPYS
1633–1703

The most famous English diarist, Samuel Pepys was a Cambridge-educated government official. He was also a bon viveur, a gourmand and a brutally honest writer. Despite writing for only ten years, his diaries cover some of the most tumultuous events of the seventeenth century, from the restoration of the monarchy to the Great Fire of London. Their joy lies in the juxtaposition of nationally significant events with the minutiae of everyday life, all narrated by a man who took an effervescent delight in living.

These extracts are typical; visitors, visits, business, and checking to see if people are still alive after the plague. Then there is the groping, in which Pepys revelled while also agonizing over (early published versions omitted many references to sex). Food is everywhere, including, here, anchovies, a newish introduction from Spain. The sweet-sour flavours of medieval cookery were starting to yield to more savoury tastes. The neat's tongue referred to is that of a calf.

from *The Diary of Samuel Pepys*

1660-61. At the end of the last and the beginning of this year, I do live in one of the houses belonging to the Navy Office, as one of the principal officers, and have done now about half a year. After much trouble with workmen I am now almost settled; my family being, myself, my wife, Jane, Will. Hewer, and Wayneman, my girle's brother. Myself in constant good health, and in a most handsome and thriving condition. Blessed be Almighty God for it. I am now taking of my sister to come and live with me. As to things of State.—The King settled, and loved of all. The Duke of York matched to my Lord Chancellor's daughter, which do not please many. The Queen upon her return to France with the Princess Henrietta. The Princess of Orange lately dead, and we into new mourning for her. We have been lately frighted with a great plot, and many taken up on it, and the fright not quite over. The Parliament, which had done all this great good to the King, beginning to grow factious, the King did dissolve it December 29th last, and another likely to be chosen speedily. I take myself now to be worth £300 clear in money, and all my goods and all manner of debts paid, which are none at all.

1660-61. January 1st. Called up this morning by

Mr. Moore, who brought me my last things for me to sign for the last month, and to my great comfort tells me that my fees will come to £80 clear to myself, and about £25 for him, which he hath got out of the pardons, though there be no fee due to me at all out of them. Then comes in my brother Thomas, and after him my father, Dr. Thomas Pepys, my uncle Fenner and his two sons (Anthony's only child dying this morning, yet he was so civil to come, and was pretty merry) to breakfast; and I had for them a barrel of oysters, a dish of neat's tongues, and a dish of anchovies, wine of all sorts, and Northdown ale. We were very merry till about eleven o'clock, and then they went away. At noon I carried my wife by coach to my cozen, Thomas Pepys, where we, with my father, Dr. Thomas, cozen Stradwick, Scott, and their wives, dined. Here I saw first his second wife, which is a very respectfull woman, but his dinner a sorry, poor dinner for a man of his estate, there being nothing but ordinary meat in it. To-day the King dined at a lord's, two doors from us. After dinner I took my wife to Whitehall, I sent her to Mrs. Pierce's (where we should have dined to-day), and I to the Privy Seal, where Mr. Moore took out all his money, and he and I went to Mr. Pierce's; in our way seeing the Duke of York bring his Lady this day to wait upon the Queen, the first time that ever she did since that great business; and the Queen is said to receive her now with much respect and love; and there he cast up the fees, and I told the money, by the same token one £100 bag, after I had told it, fell all about the room, and I fear I have lost some of it. That done I left my friends and went to my Lord's, but he being not come in I lodged the money with Mr. Shepley, and bade good night to Mr. Moore, and so returned to Mr. Pierce's, and there supped with them, and Mr. Pierce, the purser, and his wife and mine, where we had a calf's head carboned, but it was raw, we could not eat it, and a good hen. But she is such a slut that I do not love her victualls. After supper I sent them home by coach, and I went to my Lord's and there played till 12 at night at cards at Best with J. Goods and N. Osgood, and then to bed with Mr. Shepley.

June 29th. Up betimes and to my office, and by and by to the Temple, and there appointed to meet in the evening about my business, and thence I walked home, and up and down the streets is cried mightily the great victory got by the Portugalls against the Spaniards, where 10,000 slain, 3 or 4,000 taken prisoners, with all the artillery, baggage, money, &c., and Don John of Austria forced to flee with a man or two with him, which is very great news. Thence home and at my office all the morning, and then by water to St. James's but no meeting to-day being holy day, but met Mr. Creed in the Park, and after a walk or two, discoursing his business, took leave of him in Westminster Hall, whither we walked, and then came again to the Hall and fell to talk with Mrs. Lane, and after great talk that she never went abroad with any man as she used heretofore to do, I with one word got her to go with me and to meet me at the further Rhenish wine-house, where I did give her a Lobster and do so touse her and feel her all over, making her believe how fair and good a skin she has, and indeed she has a very white thigh and leg, but monstrous fat. When weary I did give over and somebody, having seen some of our dalliance, called aloud in the street, "Sir! why do you kiss the gentlewoman so?" and flung a stone at the window, which vexed me, but I believe they could not see my touzing her, and so we broke up and I went out the back way, without being observed I think, and so she towards the Hall and I to White Hall, where taking water I to the Temple with my cozen Roger and Mr. Goldsborough to Gray's Inn to his counsel, one Mr. Rawworth, a very fine man, where it being the question whether I as executor should give a warrant to Goldsborough in my reconveying her estate back again, the mortgage being performed against all acts of the testator, but only my own, my cozen said he never heard it asked before; and the other that it was always asked, and he never heard it denied, or scrupled before, so great a distance was there in their opinions, enough to make a man forswear ever having to do with the law; so they agreed to refer it to Serjeant Maynard. So we broke up, and I by water home from the Temple, and there to Sir W. Batten and eat with him, he and his lady and Sir J. Minnes having been below to-day upon the East India men that are come in, but never tell me so, but that they have been at Woolwich and Deptford, and done great deal of business. God help them. So home and up to my lute long, and then, after a little Latin chapter with Will, to bed. But I have used of late, since my wife went, to make a bad use of my fancy with whatever woman I have a mind to, which I am ashamed of, and shall endeavour to do so no more. So to sleep.

November 24th. Up, and after doing some business at the office, I to London, and there, in my way, at my old oyster shop in Gracious Streete, bought two barrels of my fine woman of the shop, who is alive after all the plague, which now is the first observation or inquiry we make at London concerning everybody we knew before it. So to the 'Change, where very busy with several people, and mightily glad to see the 'Change so full, and hopes of another abatement still the next week. Off the 'Change I went home with Sir G. Smith to dinner, sending for one of my barrels of oysters, which were good, though come from Colchester, where the plague hath been so much. Here a very brave dinner, though no invitation; and, Lord! to see how I am treated, that come from so mean a beginning, is matter of wonder to me. But it is God's great mercy to me, and His blessing upon my taking pains, and being punctual in my dealings. After dinner Captain Cocke and I about some business, and then with my other barrel of oysters home to Greenwich, sent them by water to Mrs. Penington, while he and I landed, and visited Mr. Evelyn, where most excellent discourse with him; among other things he showed me a ledger of a Treasurer of the Navy, his great grandfather, just 100 years old; which I seemed mighty fond of, and he did present me with it, which I take as a great rarity; and he hopes to find me more, older than it. He also shewed us several letters of the old Lord of Leicester's, in Queen Elizabeth's time, under the very hand-writing of Queen Elizabeth, and Queen Mary, Queen of Scotts; and others, very venerable names. But, Lord! how poorly, methinks, they wrote in those days, and in what plain uncut paper. Thence, Cocke having sent for his coach, we to Mrs. Penington, and there sat and talked and eat our oysters with great pleasure, and so home to my lodging late and to bed.

❦

ANON.
'The Women's Petition Against Coffee', 1674

Coffee reached England in the mid-seventeenth century, and the first coffee house was founded in Oxford in 1651. By the 1670s they were an established part of urban intellectual life, open to anyone who could afford a cup (or dish) of coffee. But coffee was controversial, new and potentially dangerous, and coffee houses were even worse. Charles II tried to ban them, fearing that they provided places for his enemies to plot sedition against him.

This petition, published as a pamphlet and circulated in London, was a vicious satire highlighting the various supposed ills of coffee, but essentially all amounting to the fact that it would render a man impotent. The writer or writers were unlikely to be women, but the gendering was part of the point. It played on fear of the foreign, too, just to cover every tired old trope.

'The Women's Petition Against Coffee'

Representing to Publick Consideration the
Grand Inconveniencies accruing to their
Sex from the Excessive Use of that drying,
Enfeebling Liquor.
Presented to the Right Honorable the
Keepers of the Liberty of Venus.
By a Well-willer

To the Right Honorable the Keepers of the
Liberties of *Venus*; The Worshipful Court of *Female
Assistants*, &c.

*The Humble Petitions and Address of Several
Thousands of Buxome Good-Women, Languishing in
Extremity of Want.*

Sheweth, That since 'tis Reckon'd amongst the Glories of our Native Country, To be a *Paradise for Women*: The fame in our Apprehensions can consist in nothing more than the brisk *Activity* of our men, who in former Ages were justly esteemed the *Ablest Performers* in Christendome; But to our unspeakable Grief, we find of late a very sensible *Decay* of that true *Old English Vigor*, our *Gallants* being every way so *Frenchified*, that they are become meer

Cock-sparrows, fluttering things that come on *Sa sa*, with a world of Fury, but are not able to *stand* to it, and in the very first Charge fall down *flat* before us. Never did Men wear *greater breeches*, or carry *less* in them of any *Mettle* whatsoever. There was a glorious Dispensation ('twas surely in the Golden Age) when *Lusty Ladds* of *Seven or eight hundred* years old, *Got* Sons and Daughters; ande we have read, how a Prince of *Spain* was forced to make a Law, that Men should not Repeat the *Grand Kindness* to their Wives, above NINE times a night; but Alas! Alas! Those forwards Days are gone, The dull *Lubbers* want a *Spur* now, rather than a *Bridle*: being so far from dowing any works of *Supererregation* that we find them not capable of performing those Devoirs which their *Duty*, and our *Expectations* Exact.

The Occasion of which Insufferable *Disaster*, after a furious Enquiry, and Discussion of the Point by the Learned of the *Faculty*, we can Attribute to nothing more than the Excessive use of that Newfangled, Abominable, Heathenish Liquor called COFFEE, which Riffling Nature of her Choicest *Treasures*, and *Drying* up the *Radical Moisture*, has so *Eunucht* our Husbands, and Cripple our more kind *Gallants*, that they are become as *Impotent* as Age, and as unfruitful as those *Deserts* whence that unhappy *Berry* is said to be brought.

For the continual flipping of this pitiful drink is enough to *bewitch* Men of two and twenty, and tie up the *Codpiece-points* without a Charm. It renders them that use it as *Lean* as Famine, as Rivvel'd as *Envy*, or an old meager Hagg over-ridden by an Incubus. They come from it with nothing *moist* but their snotty Noses, nothing *stiffe* but their Joints, nor *standing* but their Ears: They pretend 'twill keep them *Waking*, but we find by scurvy Experience, they *sleep quietly* enough after it. A Betrothed *Queen* might trust her self a bed with one of them, without the nice Caution of a *sword* between them: nor can call all the Art we use revive them from this Lethargy, so unfit they are for Action, that like young Train-band-men when called upon Duty, their *Ammunition* is wanting; peradventure they *Present*, but cannot give *Fire*, or at least do but *flash in the Pan*, instead of doing executions.

Nor let any Doating, Superstitious *Catos* shake their Goatish *Beards*, and task us of *Immodesty* for this Declaration, since 'tis a publick Grievance, and cries alound for Reformation. *Weight* and *Measure*, 'tis well known, should go throughout the world, and there is no torment like Famishment. Experience witnesses our Damage, and Necessity (which easily supersedes all the Laws of Decency) justifies our complaints: For can any Woman of *Sense* or *Spirit* endure with Patience, that when priviledg'd by Legal Ceremonies, she approaches the Nuptial Bed, expecting a Man that with *Sprightly* Embraces, should Answer the Vigour of her Flames, she on the contrary should only meat *A Bedful of Bones*, and hug a meager useless Corpse rendred as *sapless* as a *Kixe*, and dryer than a *Pumice-Stone*, by the perpetual Fumes of *Tobacco*, and bewitching effects of this most pernitious COFFEE, where by Nature is Enfeebled, the Off-spring of our Mighty Ancestors *Dwindled* into a Succession of *Apes* and *Pigmies*: and

— *The Age of Man*
Now Cramp't into an Inch, that was a Span.

Nor is this (though more than enough!) *All* the ground of our Complaint: For besides, we have reason to apprehend and grow *Jealous*, That Men by frequenting these *Stygian Tap-houses* will usurp on our Prerogative of *tattling*, and soon learn to exceed us in *Talkativeness*: a Quality wherein our Sex has ever Claimed preheminence: For here like so many *Frogs* in a *puddle*, they sup muddy water, and murmur insignificant notes till half a dozen of them *out-babble* an equal number of us at a *Gossipping*, talking all at once in Confusion, and running from point to point as insensibly, and swiftly, as ever the Ingenous

26

Pole-wheel could run divisions on the Base-viol; yet in all their prattle every one abounds in his own sense, as stiffly as a Quaker at the late *Barbican* Dispute, and submits to the Reasons of no other mortal: so that there being neither *Moderator* nor *Rules* observ'd, you may as soon fill a Quart pot with *Syllogismes*, as profit by their Discourses.

Certainly our Countrymens pallates are become as *Fantastical* as their Brains; how ellse is't possible they should *Apostatize* from the good old primitve way of Ale-drinking, to run a *whoring* after such variety of distructive *Foreign* Liquors, to trifle away their *time*, scald their *Chops*, and spend their *Money*, all for a little *base, black, thick, nasty, bitter, stinking, nauseous* Puddle-water: Yet (as all Witches have their Charms) so this ugly *Turskish* Enchantress by certain *Invisible Wyres* attracts both Rich and Poor; so that those that have scarce *Twopence* to buy their Children *Bread*, must spend a penny each evening in this *Insipid* Stuff: Nor can we send one of our Husbands to *Call a Midwife*, or borrow a *Glister-pipe*, but he must stay an hour by the way drinking his two *Dishes*, & two Pipes.

Daniel Defoe
1660–1731

Failed businessman, political agitator and dedicated public explainer, Daniel Defoe was a prolific writer of both novels, guidance books and political tracts. His work spans many genres and styles and was written for many different clients, as well as independently. *Robinson Crusoe*, his first novel, wove together a number of his beliefs and explored topics as varied as religious instruction, personal responsibility and colonial governance. It was also a fast-paced read that mixed travelogue with adventure and it was instantly successful.

This extract shows Crusoe exploring the island, discovering crops which would be familiar as exotic imports to his readership. Melons could be grown in the UK, but only under glass, as with citrus. Cocoa and sugar cane were very much crops of the Caribbean. The nascent British Empire already included a number of Caribbean islands which were planted with both crops, and increasingly dependent upon slave labour.

from *Robinson Crusoe*

I had been now in this unhappy island above ten months; all possibility of deliverance from this condition seemed to be entirely taken from me; and I firmly believed that no human shape had ever set foot upon that place. Having now secured my habitation, as I thought, fully to my mind, I had a great desire to make a more perfect discovery of the island, and to see what other productions I might find, which I yet knew nothing of.

It was the 15th July that I began to take a more particular survey of the island itself. I went up the creek first, where, as I hinted, I brought my rafts on shore. I found, after I came about two miles up, that the tide did not flow any higher, and that it was no more than a little brook of running water, and very fresh and good; but this being the dry season, there was hardly any water in some parts of it, at least, not enough to run in any stream, so as it could be perceived.

On the bank of this brook I found many pleasant savannas or meadows, plain, smooth, and covered with grass; and on the rising parts of them, next to the higher grounds, where the water, as might be supposed, never overflowed, I found a great deal of tobacco, green, and growing to a great and very

29

strong stalk. There were diverse other plants, which I had no notion of, or understanding about, and might perhaps have virtues of their own, which I could not find out.

I searched for the cassava root, which the Indians, in all that climate, make their bread of, but I could find none. I saw large plants of aloes, but did not then understand them. I saw several sugar-canes, but wild, and, for want of cultivation, imperfect. I contented myself with these discoveries for this time, and came back, musing with myself what course I might take to know the virtue and goodness of any of the fruits or plants which I should discover; but could bring it to no conclusion; for, in short, I had made so little observation while I was in the Brazils, that I knew little of the plants in the field, at least very little that might serve me to any purpose now in my distress.

The next day, the 16th, I went up the same way again; and after going something farther than I had gone the day before, I found the brook and the savannas began to cease, and the country became more woody than before. In this part I found different fruits, and particularly I found melons upon the ground in great abundance, and grapes upon the trees. The vines had spread indeed over the trees, and the clusters of grapes were just now in their prime, very ripe and rich. This was a surprising discovery, and I was exceeding glad of them; but I was warned by my experience to eat sparingly of them, remembering that when I was ashore in Barbary the eating of grapes killed several of our Englishmen, who were slaves there, by throwing them into fluxes and fevers. But I found an excellent use for these grapes and that was to cure or dry them in the sun, and keep them as dried grapes or raisins are kept, which I thought would be, as indeed they were, as wholesome as agreeable to eat, when no grapes might be to be had.

I spent all that evening there, and went not back to my habitation; which, by the way, was the first night, as I might say, I had lain from home. In the night, I took my first contrivance, and got up into a tree, where I slept well; and the next morning proceeded upon my discovery, travelling near four miles, as I might judge by the length of the valley, keeping still due north, with a ridge of hills on the south and north side of me.

At the end of this march I came to an opening, where the country seemed to descend to the west; and a little spring of fresh water, which issued out of the side of the hill by me, ran the other way, that is, due east; and the country appeared so fresh, so green, so flourishing, everything being in a constant verdure or flourish of spring, that it looked like a planted garden.

I descended a little on the side of that delicious vale, surveying it with a secret kind of pleasure, though mixed with my other afflicting thoughts, to think that this was all my own; that I was king and lord of all this country indefeasibly, and had a right of possession; and, if I could convey it, I might have it in inheritance as completely as any lord of a manor in England. I saw here abundance of cocoa trees, orange, and lemon, and citron trees; but all wild, and very few bearing any fruit, at least not then. However, the green limes that I gathered were not only pleasant to eat, but very wholesome; and I mixed their juice afterwards with water, which made it very wholesome, and very cool and refreshing.

I found now I had business enough to gather and carry home; and I resolved to lay up a store, as well of grapes as limes and lemons to furnish myself for the wet season, which I knew was approaching.

In order to this, I gathered a great heap of grapes in one place, and a lesser heap in another place, and a great parcel of limes and lemons in another place; and, taking a few of each with me, I travelled homeward; and resolved to come again, and bring a bag or sack, or what I could make, to carry the rest home.

Accordingly, having spent three days in this journey, I came home (so I must now call my tent and my cave); but before I got thither, the grapes were spoiled; the richness of the fruits, and the weight of the juice, having broken them and bruised them, they were good for little or nothing: as to the limes, they were good, but I could bring but a few.

The next day, being the 19th, I went back, having made me two small bags to bring home my harvest; but I was surprised, when, coming to my heap of grapes, which were so rich and fine when I gathered them, I found them all spread about, trod to pieces, and dragged about, some here, some there, and abundance eaten and devoured. By this I concluded there were some wild creatures thereabouts, which had done this; but what they were, I knew not.

However, as I found that there was no laying them up on heaps, and no carrying them away in a sack, but that one way they would be destroyed, and the other way they would be crushed with their own weight, I took another course; for I gathered a large quantity of the grapes, and hung them up upon the out-branches of the trees, that they might cure and dry in the sun; and as for the limes and lemons, I carried as many back as I could well stand under.

JONATHAN SWIFT
1667–1745

Best known for *Gulliver's Travels*, Jonathan Swift was Dean of St Patrick's Cathedral in Dublin, as well as a satirist and novelist. His 'Directions to Servants' was published posthumously, unfinished, and falls into the category of social satire. It parodies the growing genre of conduct books, with advice ranging from the unpleasant to the immoral and absurd. However, it also provides an excellent glimpse into what was not acceptable – but possibly not uncommon – amongst servants in early-eighteenth-century Britain.

'Directions to the Cook' makes clear the gender distinction which had become established by the eighteenth century: aristocrats had always employed men, preferably French, but everyone else opted for (cheaper) women cooks. It goes on. The abuses are manifest, and deeply revealing of the inner workings of the kitchen, from spit maintenance to the different types of water.

Vails were cash tips, left by visitors to the house to be distributed amongst the servants.

'Directions to the Cook',
from 'Directions to Servants'

Although I am not ignorant that it hath been a long
time since the custom began among people of quality to keep men-cooks, and generally of the *French*
nation; yet, because my treatise is chiefly calculated
for the general run of Knights, Squires, and Gentlemen both in town and country, I shall therefore
apply to you Mrs. Cook, as a woman. However, a
great part of what I intend, may serve for either sex;
and your part naturally follows the former, because
the Butler and you are joined in interest: your vails
are generally equal, and paid when others are disappointed: you can junket together at nights upon your
own progue, when the rest of the house are a-bed;
and have it in your power to make every fellow-
servant your friend: you can give a good bit or a
good fop to the little Masters and Misses, and gain
their affections: a quarrel between you is very dangerous to you both, and will probably end in one of
you being turned off; in which fatal case, perhaps,
it will not be so easy in some time to cotton with
another. And now, Mrs. Cook, I proceed to give you
my instructions; which I desire you will get some
fellow-servant in the family to read to you constantly
one night in every week when you are going to bed,

whether you serve in town or country; for my lessons shall be fitted for both.

If your Lady forgets at supper that there is any cold meat in the house, do not you be so officious as to put her in mind: it is plain she did not want it: and if she recollects it the next day, say, she gave you no orders, and it is spent: therefore, for fear of telling a lie, dispose of it with the Butler, or any other crony, before you go to bed.

Never send up a leg of a fowl at supper, while there is a cat or a dog in the house, that can be accused for running away with it: but, if there happen to be neither, you must lay it upon the rats, or a strange greyhound.

It is ill housewifry to foul your kitchen-rubbers with wiping the bottoms of the dishes you send up, since the table-cloth will do as well, and is changed every meal.

Never clean your spits after they have been used; for the grease left upon them by meat, is the best thing to preserve them from rust; and when you make use of them again, the same grease will keep the inside of the meat moist.

If you live in a rich family, roasting and boiling are below the dignity of your office, and which it becomes you to be ignorant of; therefore leave that work wholly to the Kitchen-wench, for fear of disgracing the family you live in.

If you are employed in marketing, buy your meat as cheap as you can: but, when you bring in your accounts, be tender of your master's honour, and set down the highest rate; which, besides, is but justice, for no body can afford to sell at the same rate that he buys; and I am confident that you may charge safely: swear that you gave no more than what the Butcher and Poulterer asked. If your Lady orders you to set up a piece of meat for supper, you are not to understand that you must set it up all; therefore you may give half to yourself and the Butler.

Good Cooks cannot abide what they justly call fiddling work, where abundance of time is spent and little done: such, for instance, is the dressing small birds, requiring a world of cookery and clutter, and a second or third spit: which by the way is absolutely needless; for it will be a very ridiculous thing indeed, if a spit which is strong enough to turn a surloin of beef, should not be able to turn a lark. However, if your Lady be nice, and is afraid that a large spit will tear them, place them handsomely in the dripping-pan, where the fat of roasted mutton or beef falling on the birds, will serve to baste them, and so save both time and butter: for what Cook of any spirit would lose her time in picking larks, wheat-ears, and other small birds? Therefore, if you cannot get maids, or the young Misses to assist you, e'en make short work, and either singe or flay them; there is no great loss in the skins, and the flesh is just the same.

If you are employed in market, do not accept a treat of a beef-stake and a pot of ale from the Butcher; which I think in conscience is no better than wronging your master: but do you always take that perquisite in money, if you do not go in trust, or in poundage when you pay the bills.

The kitchen-bellows being usually out of order, with stirring the fire with the muzzle, to save the tongs and poker, borrow the bellows out of your Lady's bed-chamber; which, being least used, are commonly the best in the house: and if you happen to damage or grease them, you have a chance to have them left entirely for your own use.

Let a blackguard boy be always about the house, to send on your errands, and go to market for you on rainy days; which will save your cloaths, and make you appear more creditable to your mistress.

If your mistress allows you the kitchen-stuff, in return of her generosity, take care to boil and roast your meat sufficiently. If she keeps it for her own profit, do her justice; and rather than let a good fire be wanting, enliven it now and then with the dripping, and the butter that happens to turn to oil.

Send up your meat well stuck with scewers, to make it look round and plump; and an iron scewer rightly employed now and then, will make it look handsomer.

When you roast a long joint of meat, be careful only about the middle, and leave the two extreme parts raw; which may serve another time, and will also save firing.

When you scour your plates and dishes, bend the brim inward, so to make them hold the more.

Always keep a large fire in the kitchen, when there is a small dinner, or the family dines abroad; that the neighbours, seeing the smoak, may commend your master's house-keeping: but, when much company is invited, then be as sparing as possible of your coals; because a great deal of the meat, being half raw, will be saved, and serve next day.

Boil your meat constantly in pump-water, because you must sometimes want river or pipe water; and then your mistress, observing your meat of a different colour, will chide you when you are not in fault.

When you have plenty of fowl in the larder, leave the door open, in pity to the poor cat, if she be a good mouser.

If you find it necessary to market in a wet day,

take out your mistress's riding hood and cloak, to save your cloaths.

Get three or four Char-women to attend you constantly in the kitchen; whom you pay at small charges, only with the broken meat, a few coals, and all the cinders.

To keep troublesome servants out of the kitchen, always leave the winder sticking on the jack, to fall on their heads.

If a lump of soot falls into the soup, and you cannot conveniently get it out, stir it well, and it will give the soup a high *French taste*.

If you melt your butter to oil, be under no concern, but send it up; for oil is a genteeler sauce than butter.

Scrape the bottoms of your pots and kettles with a silver spoon, for fear of giving them a taste of copper.

When you send up butter for sauce, be so thrifty as to let it be half water; which is also much wholesomer.

If your butter, when it is melted, tastes of brass, it is your master's fault, who will not allow you a silver saucepan; besides, the less of it will go further, and new tinning is very chargeable. If you have a silver sauce-pan, and the butter smells of smoak, lay the fault upon the coals.

Never make use of a spoon in any thing that you can do with your hands, for fear of wearing out your master's plate.

When you find that you cannot get dinner ready at the time appointed, put the clock back, and then it may be ready to a minute.

Let a red-hot coal now and then fall into the dripping pan, that the smoak of the dripping may ascend, and give the roast meat a high taste.

You are to look upon your kitchen as your dressing-room: but you are not to wash your hands till you have gone to the necessary house, and spitted your meat, trussed your fowl, picked your sallad, nor indeed till after you have sent up your second course; for your hands will be ten times fouler with the many things you are forced to handle; but, when your work is over, one washing will serve for all.

There is but one part of your dressing that I would admit while the victuals are boiling, roasting, or stewing, I mean the combing your head; which loseth no time, because you can stand over your cookery, and watch it with one hand, while you are using your comb in the other.

If any of the combings happen to be sent up with the victuals, you may safely lay the fault upon any of the Footmen that hath vexed you; as those Gentlemen are sometimes apt to be malicious, if you refuse

41

them a sop in the pan, or a slice from the spit, much more when you discharge a ladle-full of hot porridge on their legs, or send them up to their masters with a dish-clout pinned at their tails.

In roasting and boiling, order the Kitchen-maid to bring none but the large coals, and save the small ones for the fires above stairs: the first are properest for dressing meat; and when they are out, if you happen to miscarry in any dish, you may lay the fault upon want of coals: besides, the Cinder-pickers will be sure to speak ill of your master's house-keeping, where they do not find plenty of large cinders mixed with fresh large coals. Thus you may dress your meat with credit, do an act of charity, raise the honour of your master, and sometimes get share of a pot of ale for your bounty to the Cinder-woman.

As soon as you have sent up the second course, you have nothing to do (in a great family) until supper: therefore scour your hands and face, put on your hood and scarf, and take your pleasure among your cronies till nine or ten at night.—But dine first.

Let there be always a strict friendship between you and the Butler: for it is both your interests to be united: the Butler often wants a comfortable tit-bit, and you much oftener a cool cup of good liquor. However, be cautious of him; for he is sometimes an inconstant lover, because he hath great advantage to allure the maids with a glass of sack, or white-wine and sugar.

When you roast a breast of veal, remember your sweet-heart the Butler loves a sweet-bread; therefore set it aside till evening, you can say, the cat or the dog has run away with it, or you found it tainted, or fly-blown; and besides, it looks as well at the table without it as with it.

When you make the company wait long for dinner, and the meat be overdone, which is generally the case, you may lawfully lay the fault upon your Lady; who hurried you so to send up dinner, that you was forced to send it up too much boiled and roasted.

If your dinner miscarries in almost every dish, how could you help it? You were teized by the Foot-men coming into the kitchen; and, to prove it true, take occasion to be angry, and throw a ladle-full of broth on one or two of their liveries. Besides, *Friday* and *Childermas-day* are two cross days in the week, and it is impossible to have good luck on either of them; therefore on those two days you have a lawful excuse.

When you are in haste to take down your dishes, tip them in such a manner, that a dozen will fall together upon the dresser, just ready for your hand.

To save time and trouble, cut your apples and onions with the same knife; and well-bred Gentry love the taste of an onion in every thing they eat.

Lump three or four pounds of butter together with your hands; then dash it against the wall just over the dresser, so as to have it ready to pull by pieces, as you have occasion for it.

If you have a silver sauce-pan for the kitchen-use, let me advise you to batter it well, and keep it always black: this will be for your master's honour; for it shews there has been constant good house-keeping. And make room for the sauce-pan by wriggling it on the coals, &c.

In the same manner, if you are allowed a large silver spoon for the kitchen, let half the bole of it be worn out with continual scraping and stirring; and often say merrily, This spoon owes my master no service.

When you send up a mess of broth, water-gruel, or the like, to your master in a morning, do not forget with your thumb and two fingers to put salt on the side of the plate; for, if you make use of a spoon, or the end of a knife, there may be danger that the salt would fall, and that would be a sign of ill luck. Only remember to lick your thumb and fingers clean, before you offer to touch the salt.

WILLIAM VERRALL
1715–1761

The Georgian period was one of prosperity and cultural change in Britain. Its trade networks spanned the globe, and once-new ingredients such as tomatoes, chillis, pineapples and potatoes were gaining acceptance. The near-eastern influenced flavours of the medieval era were forgotten, and the nouvelle cuisine of its day was French. Inevitably, there was a backlash, and French cookery was attacked for its extravagance, its complication, and its expense.

William Verrall was the master of the White Hart Inn in Lewes, but he owed his position to the Duke of Newcastle, where he'd worked under the French chef Pierre St-Clouet. At the White Hart, he offered two menus, one for the genteel palates of the Duke and his cronies, and one for the lesser folk. He also wrote a book, intended to show how great this new style was – along with how great the author was. However bad her cooking was, it is hard not to pity poor Nanny.

'Preface',
from *A Complete System of Cookery*

I have been sent for many and many a time to get
dinners for some of the best families hereabouts; the
salute generally is: Will, (for that is my name) I want
you to dress me a dinner to-day; with all my heart,
Sir, says I; how many will your company be; why
about ten or twelve, or thereabouts: and what would
you please to have me get, Sir, for ye? O, says the
gentleman, I shall leave that entirely to you; but I'll
show you my larder, and you'll be the better judge
how to make your bill of fare; and a vast plenty of
good provisions there was, enough to make two
courses, one of seven, the other of nine, with an add-
ition only of three or four small dishes for the
second course; and a fine dish of fish there was for
a remove. So it was agreed that should be the thing;
but, says the gentleman, be sure you make us some
good things in your own way, for they are polite sort
of gentry that are to dine with me. I promised my
care, and wrote the bill immediately; and it was
vastly approved of. My next step was to go and offer
a great many compliments to Mrs. Cook about getting the dinner; and as it was her master's order I
should assist her, I hoped we should agree; and the
girl, I'll say that for her, returned the compliment

very prettily, by saying, Sir, whatever my master or you shall order me to do, shall be done as far and as well as I am able. But Nanny (for that I found to be her name) soon got into such an air as often happens upon such occasions. Pray, Nanny, says I, where do you place your stewpans, and the other things you make use of in the cooking way? La, Sir, says she, that is all we have (pointing to one poor solitary stewpan, as one might call it,) but no more fit for the use than a wooden hand-dish. Ump, says I to myself, how's this to be? A surgeon may as well attempt to make an incision with a pair of sheers, or open a vein with an oyster-knife, as for me to pretend to get this dinner without proper tools to do it; here's neither stewpan, soup-pot, or any one thing else that is useful; there's what they call a frying-pan indeed, but black as my hat, and a handle long enough to obstruct half the passage of the kitchen. However, upon a little pause I sent away post haste for my own kitchen furniture. In the meantime Nanny and I kept on in preparing what we could, that no time might be lost. When the things came we at it again, and all was in a tolerable way, and forward enough for the time of day; but at length wanting a sieve I begg'd of Nanny to give me one, and so she did in a moment; but such a one!—I put my fingers to it and found it gravelly. Nanny, says I, this won't do, it is sandy: she look'd at it, and angry enough she was: rot our Sue, says she, she's always taking my sieve to sand her nasty dirty stairs. But, however, to be a little cleanly Nanny gave it a good thump upon the table, much about the part of it where the meat is generally laid, and whips it into the boiler where I suppose the pork and cabbage was boiling for the family, gives it a sort of a rinse, and gave it me again, with as much of the pork fat about it as would poison the whole dinner; so I said no more, but could not use it, and made use of a napkin that I slily made friends with her fellow-servant for; at which she leer'd round and set off; but I heard her say as she flirted her tail into the scullery, hang these men cooks, they are so confounded nice.—I'll be whipt, says she, if there was more sand in the sieve than would lay upon a sixpence. However, she came again presently, and I soon coax'd her into good humour again; come, says I, Nanny, I'm going to make a fricasee of chickens, observe how I cut 'em (for I'll show ye how to do any part of the dinner), and she seemed very attentive. When I had cut mine, there, says I, do you take that, and cut it in the same manner: and indeed the girl handled her knife well, and did it very prettily: then I gave her directions how to proceed; and it was done neatly, notwithstanding the story of the sandy sieve. I then took in hand to show her in what manner it was to be finished for the table. And now, dinner being dish'd up, Nanny was vastly pleased, and said, that in her judgment it was the prettiest and best she had ever seen. When 'twas over, the gentleman desired, if I had time in the evening, he should be glad I would come and get him two or three little matters for supper, for they all stay: and be sure, says he, make us just such another fricasee, for it was highly approved on; so I went and told Nanny she should do it; which was agreed to: but, Sir, says she, if I don't do right I hope you'll tell me. But it was done to my mind, and Nanny was now the cook; supper was sent in, and great praises ran from plate to plate, and they unanimously agreed that that fricasee was better than what they had for dinner. Before supper was well over out comes the gentleman to me. Will, says he, we hope you have this dish in the book you are going to publish. Yes, Sir, says I, and everything else you had to-day drest in the foreign way. But, Sir, says I, your cook did that you had for supper. My maid do it, says he, and away he went to his company. Nanny was immediately sent for, and after some questions something was given her for the care she had taken; so I wished the family a good night, and went home.

ELIZABETH RAFFALD
1733–1781

Trained as a cook and eventually rising to house-keeper, Elizabeth Raffald was an entrepreneur, caterer, and author of one of the best cookery books of the eighteenth century. After leaving service on marriage, she worked as an innkeeper, kept a servants' registry, ran a cookery school and a coffee shop. Her marriage was not a success, and her husband was an alcoholic.

The Experienced English Housekeeper was aimed at the upper-middle class and those who cooked for them. Unusually for the time, it was based on original recipes, drawn from her own experience, clearly written and easy to follow. It was entirely culinary, which was also unusual (usually medicine and perfumery slipped in too), and the fantastical recipes for jellies, blancmanges and sugarwork are still jaw-dropping when cooked today. This recipe relies on specialist moulds, which make it hard to replicate now. Flummery was a type of blancmange.

'Hen and Chickens in Jelly',
from *The Experienced English Housekeeper*

Make some flummery with a deal of sweet almonds in it, colour a little of it brown with chocolate and put it in a mould the shape of a hen. Then colour some more flummery with the yolk of a hard egg beat as fine as possible, leave part of your flummery white. Then fill the moulds of seven chickens, three with white flummery and three with yellow, and one the colour of the hen. When they are cold turn them into a deep dish, put under and round them lemon peel boiled tender and cut like straw. Then put a little clear calf's foot jelly under them to keep them in their places, and let it stand till it is stiff. Then fill up your dish with more jelly.

They are a pretty decoration for a grand table.

ROBERT BURNS
1759–1796

Probably the most famous Scottish poet, Robert Burns started life as a farm labourer and remained a farmer for most of his life. His career as a poet was cut short by his death at the age of thirty-seven, at which time he was working as an excise officer as well as writing. However, as the composer of 'Auld Lang Syne' and one of the earliest proponents of Scottish-authored and distinctively voiced verse and songs, his fame grew after his death to the point where he was voted the greatest Scot in a poll of 2009.

'Address to a Haggis' is triumphantly Scottish, but also contains some of the tropes of the wider British food scene. Verses 5 to 6 include a dig at French food and also point up the contrast between the fashionable rich man and the romanticized version of the rural peasant.

'Address to a Haggis'

Fair fa' your honest, sonsie face,
Great Chieftain o' the Puddin-race!
Aboon them a' ye tak your place,
    Painch, tripe, or thairm:
Weel are ye wordy o' a *grace*
    As lang's my arm.

The groaning trencher there ye fill,
Your hurdies like a distant hill,
Your *pin* wad help to mend a mill
    In time o' need,
While thro' your pores the dews distil
    Like amber bead.

His knife see Rustic-labour dight,
An' cut you up wi' ready slight,
Trenching your gushing entrails bright,
    Like onie ditch;
And then, O what a glorious sight,
    Warm-reekin, rich!

Then, horn for horn, they stretch an' strive:
Deil tak the hindmost, on they drive,
Till a' their weel-swall'd kytes belyve
    Are bent like drums;
Then auld Guidman, maist like to rive,
    Bethankit hums.

Is there that owre his French *ragout*,
Or *olio* that wad staw a sow,
Or *fricassee* wad mak her spew
        Wi' perfect scunner,
Looks down wi' sneering, scornfu' view
        On sic a dinner?

Poor devil! see him owre his trash,
As feckless as a wither'd rash,
His spindle shank a guid whip-lash,
        His nieve a nit;
Thro' bluidy flood or field to dash,
        O how unfit!

But mark the Rustic, *haggis-fed*,
The trembling earth resounds his tread,
Clap in his walie nieve a blade,
        He'll make it whissle;
An' legs, an' arms, an' heads will sned,
        Like taps o' thrissle.

Ye Pow'rs wha mak mankind your care,
And dish them out their bill o' fare,
Auld Scotland wants nae skinking ware
        That jaups in luggies;
But, if ye wish her gratefu' prayer,
        Gie her a *Haggis*!

James Boswell
1740–1795

Samuel Johnson, one of the great literary figures of the eighteenth century, was the subject of a biography by his friend, admirer and travel companion, James Boswell, which in its turn has become one of the most famous British biographies. Johnson was a polarizing figure: praised for his intellect, quick wit and vast knowledge, he gave a terrible first impression. Scarred by operations and illness as a child, he also suffered from physical convulsions which may have been caused by Tourette's syndrome. He could also be a cutting critic and he was something of a glutton.

As this rather brutal passage from Boswell's *Life of Samuel Johnson* illustrates, those who invited Johnson to dinner in the hope of scintillating conversation might well be disappointed. Late-eighteenth-century meals could be gargantuan, with tens of dishes all laid out on the table simultaneously, inviting excess. The mark of politeness was to show restraint. Presumably, all that intellect had to be fuelled from somewhere.

from Boswell's *Life of Samuel Johnson*

At supper this night he talked of good eating with uncommon satisfaction. 'Some people (said he,) have a foolish way of not minding, or pretending not to mind, what they eat. For my part, I mind my belly very studiously, and very carefully; for I look upon it, that he who does not mind his belly will hardly mind anything else.' He now appeared to me *Jean Bull philosophe*, and he was, for the moment, not only serious but vehement. Yet I have heard him, upon other occasions, talk with great contempt of people who were anxious to gratify their palates; and the 206th number of his *Rambler* is a masterly essay against gulosity. His practice, indeed, I must acknowledge, may be considered as casting the balance of his different opinions upon this subject; for I never new knew any man who relished good eating more than he did. When at table, he was totally absorbed in the business of the moment; his looks seemed rivetted to his plate; nor would he, unless when in very high company, say one word, or even pay the least attention to what was said by others, till he had satisfied his appetite, which was so fierce, and indulged with such intenseness, that while in the act of eating, the veins of his forehead swelled, and generally a strong perspiration was visible. To those whose sensations were delicate, this could not but be disgusting; and it was doubtless not very suitable to the character of a philosopher, who should be distinguished by self-command. But it must be owned, that Johnson, though he could be rigidly *abstemious*, was not a *temperate* man either in eating or drinking. He could refrain, but he could not use moderately. He told me, that he had fasted two days without inconvenience, and that he had never been hungry but once. They who beheld with wonder how much he eat upon all occasions when his dinner was to his taste, could not easily conceive what he must have meant by hunger; and not only was he remarkable for the extraordinary quantity which he eat, but he was, or affected to be, a man of very nice discernment in the science of cookery. He used to descant critically on the dishes which had been at table where he had dined or supped, and to recollect very minutely what he had liked. I remember, when he was in Scotland, his praising '*Gordon's palates,*' (a dish of palates at the Honourable Alexander Gordon's) with a warmth of expression which might have done honour to more important subjects. 'As for Maclaurin's imitation of a *made dish*, it was a wretched attempt.' He about the same time was so much displeased with the performances of a nobleman's French cook, that he exclaimed with vehemence, 'I'd throw such a rascal into the river; and he then proceeded to alarm a lady at whose house he was to sup, by the following manifesto of his skill: 'I, Madam, who live at a variety of good tables, am a much better judge of cookery, than any person who has a very tolerable cook, but lives much at home; for his palate is gradually adapted to the taste of his cook; whereas, Madam, in trying by a wider range, I can more exquisitely judge.' When invited to dine, even with an intimate friend, he was not pleased if something better than a plain dinner was not prepared for him. I have heard him say on such an occasion, 'This was a good dinner enough, to be sure; but it was not a dinner to *ask* a man to.' On the other hand, he was wont to express, with great glee, his satisfaction when he had been entertained quite to his mind. One day when we had dined with his neighbour and landlord in Bolt-court, Mr. Allen, the printer, whose old housekeeper had studied his taste in every thing, he pronounced this eulogy: 'Sir, we could not have had a better dinner had there been a *Synod of Cooks.*'

WILLIAM KITCHINER
1775–1827

William Kitchiner was a classic learned Georgian man of leisure. He faked his academic credentials, claiming a medical degree from Glasgow, but was nevertheless knowledgeable and enthusiastic, and elected a fellow of the Royal Society for his work on optics. He also wrote operettas and several culinary works, including *The Cook's Oracle*, based, at least partially, on his own experiences in the kitchen, including washing up and shopping.

The *Oracle* at times verges on the slightly crazed, with extended discourses, as here, on tangential topics, or puffing particular products or ideas. Kitchiner blended thoughts on medicine, flavour and practicality with a flare which ensured that the book would be a bestseller both in the UK and also in the US, where it was published in 1822 and went into multiple editions.

from *The Cook's Oracle*

To chew long, and leisurely, is the only way to extract the quintessence of our food, to completely enjoy the taste of it, and to render it easily convertible into laudable chyle, by the facility it gives to the gastric juices to dissolve it without trouble. The pleasure of the palate, and the health of the stomach, are equally promoted by this salutary habit, which all should be taught to acquire in their infancy. The more tender the meat is, the more we may eat of it. From thirty to forty (according to the tenderness of the meat) may be given as the mean number of munches, that solid meat requires, to prepare it for its journey down the *red lane*, less will be sufficient for tender, delicate, and easily digestible white meats. The sagacious *gourmand*, must calculate this precisely, and not waste his precious moments in useless jaw-work, or invite an indigestion by neglecting mastication. I cannot give any rules for this, as it depends so much on the strength or weakness of the subject, especially the state of the Teeth and maxillary glands; every one ought to ascertain the condition of these useful working tools, and to use them with proportionate diligence is an indispensable exercise which every rational epicure will cheerfully perform, who has a proper regard for the welfare of his stomach. The

Teeth should be cleaned after each meal with a "TOOTH PRESERVER," (*i. e.* a very soft brush,) and then rinsed with tepid water—especially, *never neglect this at night*; nothing destroys the Teeth so fast as suffering animal food to stick between them. It is the rage now with many Dentists to recommend brushes so hard, that they fetch blood like a lancet wherever they touch, and instead of "TEETH PRESERVERS," may be called very properly "GUM BLEEDERS."

Mastication is the source of all good digestion; with it, almost any thing may be put into any stomach with impunity: without it, digestion must be always difficult, and frequently impossible: and be it remembered, it is not merely what we eat, but what we digest well, that nourishes us. The sagacious *gourmand* is ever mindful of his motto,

"*Masticate, denticate, chump, grind, and swallow,*"

The four first acts of which he knows he must perform well, before he dare attempt the fifth."

N. B. PATENT MASTICATORS, may be had of Palmer, entler, in St. James's-street.

CHARLES LAMB
1775–1834

Known mainly as an essayist, Charles Lamb was part of a literary circle which included Samuel Coleridge, William Wordsworth and Robert Southey, among others. He wrote poetry and prose, for both adults and children, often collaborating with his sister Mary. However, he is best known for his essays which cover a wide range of topics, drawing on his own experiences as well as telling stories and generally musing.

His *Dissertation Upon Roast Pig* tells of the supposed discovery that roast pork was a thing of glory, when a swineherd accidentally burnt his house down with his pigs within it and, while picking through the remains, licked his fingers. This section is both an ode to a delicious morsel, and a sly poke at upper-class tables, upon which roast pork was decidedly uncommon.

from *A Dissertation Upon Roast Pig*

Without placing too implicit faith in the account above given, it must be agreed, that if a worthy pretext for so dangerous an experiment as setting houses on fire (especially in these days) could be assigned in favour of any culinary object, that pretext and excuse might be found in roast pig.

Of all the delicacies in the whole *mundus edibilis*, I will mantain it to be the most delicate — *princeps obsoniorum*.

I speak not of your grown porkers — things between pig and pork — those hobbydehoys — but a young and tender suckling — under a moon old — guiltless as yet of the sty — with no original speck of the *amor immunditia*, the hereditary failing of the first parent, yet manifest — his voice as yet not broken, but something between a childish treble, and a grumble — the mild forerunner, or *praludium*, of a grunt.

He must be roasted. I am not ignorant that our ancestors ate them seethed, or boiled — but what a sacrifice of the exterior tegument!

There is no flavour comparable, I will contend, to that of the crisp, tawny, well-watched, not over-roasted, *crackling*, as it is well called — the very teeth are invited to their share of the pleasure at this banquet in overcoming the coy, brittle resistance — with the adhesive oleaginous — O call it not fat — but an indefiable sweetness growing up to it — the tender blossoming of fat — fat cropped in the bud — taken in the shoot — in the first innocence — the cream and quintessence of the child-pig's yet pure food — the lean, no lean, but a kind of animal manna — or, rather, fat and lean (if it must be so) so blended and running into each other, that both together make but one ambrosian result, or common substance.

Behold him, while he is doing — it seemeth rather a refreshing warmth, then a scorching heat, that he is so passive to. How equably he twirleth round the string! — Now he is just done. To see the extreme sensibility of that tender age, he hath wept out his pretty eyes — radiant jellies — shooting stars —

See him in the dish, his second cradle, how meek he lieth! — wouldst thou have had this innocent grow up to the grossness and indocility which too often accompany maturer swinehood? Ten to one he would have proved a glutton, a sloven, an obstinate, disagreeable animal — wallowing in all manner of filthy conversation — from these sins he is happily snatched away —

Ere sin could blight, or sorrow fade,
Death came with timely care —

his memory is odoriferous — no clown curseth, while his stomach half rejecteth, the rank bacon — no coalheaver bolteth him in reeking sausages — he hath a fair sepulchre in the grateful stomach of the judicious epicure — and for such a tomb might be content to die.

He is the best of sapors. Pineapple is great. She is indeed almost too transcendent — a delight, if not sinful, yet so like to sinning, that really a tender-conscienced person would do well to pause — too ravishing for mortal taste, she woundeth and excoriateth the lips that approach her — like lover's kisses, she biteth — she is a pleasure bordering on pain from the fierceness and insanity of her relish — but she stoppeth at the palate — she meddleth not with the appetite — and the coarsest hunger might barter her consistently for a mutton chop.

Pig — let me speak his praise — is no less provocative of the appetite, than he is satisfactory to the criticalness of the censorious palate. The strong man may batten on him, and the weakling refuseth not his mild juices.

Unlike to mankind's mixed characters, a bundle of virtues and vices, inexplicably intertwisted, and not to be unravelled without hazard, he is — good throughout. No part of him is better or worse than another. He helpeth, as far as his little means extend, all around. He is the least envious of banquets. He is all neighbors' fare.

I am one of those, who freely and ungrudgingly impart a share of the good things of this life which fall to their lot (few as mine are in this kind) to a friend. I protest I take as great an interest in my friend's pleasures, his relishes, and proper satisfactions, as in mine own. "Presents," I often say, "endear Absents." Hares, pheasants, partridges, snipes, barn-door chickens (those "tame villatic fowl"), capons, plovers, brawn, barrels of oysters, I dispense as freely as I receive them. I love to taste them, as it were, upon the tongue of my friend. But a stop must be put somewhere. One would not, like Lear, "give everything." I make my stand upon pig. Methinks it is an ingratitude to the Giver of all good flavours, to extra-domiciliate, or send out of the house, slightingly (under pretext of friendship, or I know not what), a blessing so particularly adapted, predestined, I may say, to my individual palate — It argues an insensibility.

WALTER SCOTT
1771–1832

Walter Scott was a lawyer as well as a prolific and very popular writer. A key figure in defining Scottishness, he was concerned with the idea of Scotland as a cultural entity, for at the time it had few independent political institutions. He was well-connected, organizing the visit of George IV to Scotland in 1822, at which the king appeared in flesh-coloured tights and a kilt, and the parades were a sea of tartan.

Often credited with inventing the historic novel, Scott gave *Saint Ronan's Well* a vaguely contemporary setting, one of only three novels to be set in his lifetime. It was a tragedy, revolving around false promises, secret marriages and profligacy, and was not well-received at the time. However, the character of Med Dods, the innkeeper of the town's hostelry, captured the imagination of many, and today the novel is associated more with her than the plot itself.

from *Saint Ronan's Well*

The worthy couple (servants and favorites of the Mowbray family) who first kept the inn, had died reasonably wealthy, after long carrying on a flourishing trade, leaving behind them an only daughter. They had acquired by degrees not only the property of the inn itself, of which they were originally tenants, but of some remarkably good meadow-land by the side of the brook, which, when touched by a little pecuniary necessity, the Lairds of St. Ronan's had disposed of piecemeal, as the readiest way to portion off a daughter, procure a commission for the younger son, and the like emergencies. So that Meg Dods, when she succeeded to her parents, was a considerable heiress, and, as such, had the honor of refusing three topping farmers, two bonnet-lairds, and a horse-couper, who successively made proposals to her.

Many bets were laid on the horse-couper's success, but the knowing ones were taken in. Determined to ride the forehorse herself, Meg would admit no helpmate who might soon assert the rights of a master; and so, in single blessedness, and with the despotism of Queen Bess herself, she ruled all matters with a high hand, not only over her menservants and maid-servants, but over the stranger within her gates, who, if he ventured to oppose Meg's sovereign will and pleasure, or desired to have either fare or accommodation different from that which she chose to provide for him, was instantly ejected with that answer which Erasmus tells us silenced all complaints in the German inns of his time, *Quare aliud hospitium,* or, as Meg expressed it, "Troop aff wi' ye to another public." As this amounted to a banishment in extent equal to sixteen miles from Meg's residence, the unhappy party on whom it was passed had no other refuge save by deprecating the wrath of his landlady, and re-signing himself to her will. It is but justice to Meg Dods to state, that though hers was a severe and almost despotic government, it could not be termed a tyranny, since it was exercised upon the whole for the good of the subject.

The vaults of the old Laird's cellar had not, even in his own day, been replenished with more excellent wines; the only difficulty was to prevail on Meg to look for the precise liquor you chose;—to which it may be added, that she often became restive when she thought a company had had "as much as did them good," and refused to furnish any more supplies. Then her kitchen was her pride and glory; she looked to the dressing of every dish herself, and there were some with which she suffered no one to interfere. Such were the cock-a-leeky, and the savory minced collops, which rivaled in their way even the veal cutlets of our old friend Mrs. Hall, at Ferrybridge. Meg's table-linen, bed-linen, and so forth, were always home made, of the best quality, and in the best order; and a weary day was that to the chambermaid in which her lynx eye discovered any neglect of the strict cleanliness which she constantly enforced. Indeed, considering Meg's country and calling, we were never able to account for her extreme and scrupulous nicety, unless by supposing that it afforded her the most apt and frequent pretext for scolding her maids; an exercise in which she displayed so much eloquence and energy, that we must needs believe it to have been a favorite one.

We have only further to commemorate the moderation of Meg's reckonings, which, when they closed the banquet, often relieved the apprehensions, instead of saddening the heart, of the rising guest. A shilling for breakfast, three shillings for dinner, including a pint of old port, eighteenpence for a snug supper—such were the charges of the inn at St. Ronan's, under this landlady of the olden world, even after the nineteenth century had commenced; and they were ever tendered with the pious recollection, that her good father never charged half so much, but these weary times rendered it impossible for her to make the lawing less.

Notwithstanding all these excellent and rare properties, the inn at St. Ronan's shared the decay of the village to which it belonged. This was owing to various circumstances. The high-road had been turned aside from the place, the steepness of the street being murder (so the postilions declared) to their post-horses. It was thought that Meg's stern refusal to treat them with liquor, or to connive at their exchanging for porter and whisky the corn which should feed their cattle, had no small influence on the opinion of those respectable gentlemen, and that a little cutting and leveling would have made the ascent easy enough; but let that pass. This alteration of the highway was an injury which Meg did not easily forgive to the country gentlemen, most of whom she had recollected when children. "Their fathers," she said, "wad not have done the like of it to a lone woman." Then the decay of the village itself, which had formerly contained a set of feuars and bonnet-lairds, who, under the name of the Chirupping Club, contrived to drink twopenny, qualified with brandy or whisky, at least twice or thrice a week, was some small loss.

The temper and manners of the landlady scared away all customers of that numerous class, who will not allow originality to be an excuse for the breach of decorum, and who, little accustomed perhaps to attendance at home, love to play the great man at an inn, and to have a certain number of bows, deferential speeches, and apologies, in answer to the G—d—n ye's which they bestow on the house, attendance, and entertainment. Unto those who commenced this sort of barter in the Clachan of St. Ronan's, well could Meg Dods pay it back, in their own coin; and glad they were to escape from the house with eyes not quite scratched out, and ears not more deafened than if they had been within hearing of a pitched battle.

Nature had formed honest Meg for such encounters; and as her noble soul delighted in them, so her outward properties were in what Tony Lumpkin calls a concatenation accordingly. She had hair of a brindled color, betwixt black and gray, which was apt to escape in elf-locks from under her mutch when she was thrown into violent agitation—long skinny hands, terminated by stout talons—gray eyes, thin lips, a robust person, a broad, though flat chest, capital wind, and a voice that could match a choir of fish-women. She was accustomed to say of herself, in her more gentle moods, that her bark was worse than her bite; but what teeth could have matched a tongue, which, when in full career, is vouched to have been heard from the Kirk to the Castle of St. Ronan's?

These notable gifts, however, had no charms for the travelers of these light and giddy-paced times, and Meg's inn became less and less frequented. What carried the evil to the uttermost was, that a fanciful lady of rank in the neighborhood chanced to recover of some imaginary complaint by the use of a mineral well about a mile and a half from the village; a fashionable doctor was found to write an analysis of the healing waters, with a list of sundry cures; a speculative builder took land in feu, and erected lodging-houses, shops, and even streets. At length a tontine subscription was obtained to erect an inn, which, for the more grace, was called a hotel; and so the desertion of Meg Dods became general.

She had still, however, her friends and well-wishers, many of whom thought, that as she was a lone woman, and known to be well to pass in the world, she would act wisely to retire from public life, and take down a sign which had no longer fascination for guests. But Meg's spirit scorned submission direct or implied. "Her father's door," she said, "should be open to the road, till her father's bairn should be streekit and carried out at it with her feet foremost. It was not for the profit—there was little profit at it;—profit?—there was a dead loss;—but she wad not be dung by any of them. They maun hae a hottle, maun they?—and an honest public canna serve them! They may hottle that likes; but they shall see that Lucky Dods can hottle on as lang as the best of them—ay, though they had made a Tamteen of it, and linkit a' their breaths of lives, whilk are in their nostrils, on end of ilk other like a string of wild geese, and the langest liver bruick a' (whilk was sinful presumption), she would match ilk ane of them, as lang as her ain wind held out." Fortunate it was for Meg, since she had formed this doughty resolution, that although her inn had decayed in custom, her land had risen in value in a degree which more than compensated the balance on the wrong side of her books, and, joined to her usual providence and economy, enabled her to act up to her lofty purpose.

❦

CHRISTIAN ISOBEL JOHNSTONE &
WALTER SCOTT
1781–1857 and 1771–1832

Six years after the publication of *Saint Ronan's Well*, a spin-off cookery book appeared. *The Cook and Housewife's Manual* rapidly became a bestseller in its own right. It was hailed as a true Scottish cookery book, and although by no means the first Scottish-authored recipe book, in its overt Scottishness it echoes the cultural awakening that Scott was so keen to promote. Its author, Christian Isobel Johnstone, was a journalist and editor, the only woman to edit a leading periodical at the time.

The introduction to the book, which contained a mixture of English, French(ish) and explicitly Scottish recipes, was possibly written by Walter Scott, who thought the book so good that he wrote it into a later edition of *Saint Ronan's Well*. It uses characters from the novel, gathering at the inn as part of a dining club. This extract shows them decrying fashionable French food in favour of good old-fashioned Scottish fare.

from *The Cook and Housewife's Manual*

Nothing was farther from the real intention of Dr. Redgill than to refuse an invitation, which the savoury steams, now issuing from Meg's kitchen—"steams that might have created a stomach under the ribs of death"—rendered irresistibly seductive. With a decent show of hesitation, he yielded; and, snuffing up the incense-breathing vapours which ascended the stair, followed the Nabob to a private parlour, where an old, rich china basin, filled with the balmy and ambrosial fluid, was twice replenished for his solace; first, however, improved by a pin's-point of crystals of Cayenne from a silver pocket-case of essence vials, which had luckily escaped the taint of the stye.

"Excellent hare-soup—very excellent indeed I pronounce it, Mr. Touchwood. All the blood preserved—the consistence—the concoction complete—the seasoning admirable. Sir, I abhor the injustice of withholding from the poor cook the praise that is her due. It is bad policy, Mr. Touchwood. This hare-soup, I say again, is excellent; and, to my thinking, though a Scottish mode, the very best way of dressing a hare. Sir, you are in snug quarters here. A sensible, discreet person, your hostess, though a little gruff at the first brush. Sir, all good cooks are so. They know their own value—they are a privileged class—they toil in a fiery element—they lie under a heavy responsibility. But, perhaps, after all, you travel with your own cook—many gentlemen who have travelled do."

"No such thing," replied Touchwood; "never less alone than when alone in affairs of the stomach. I may have written out a few items for my old dame here, and taken a peep occasionally into the kitchen and larder for the first three months; but now, matters go on as smoothly as oiled butter."

"Sir, you write receipts, then!" cried the Doctor, looking on his hospitable entertainer with augmented respect,—"perhaps for this very soup—and perhaps—but it would be too great a kindness to request on such short acquaintance—though hare-soup, sir, I will candidly own it, is only understood in Scotland. Sir, I am above national prejudices; and, I must say, I yield the Scots the Superiority in all soups—save turtle and mullagatawny. An anti-quarian friend of mine attributes this to their early and long connexion with the French, a nation emi-nent in soups."

"No doubt of it, Doctor," replied the Nabob; "but you shall have this receipt, ay and twenty more receipts. To this ancient hostel now—you will scarce believe it—have been confined scores of admirable receipts in cookery, ever since the jolly friars flourished down in the Monastery yonder:

"The Monks of Melrose made fat kail
On Fridays, when they fasted."

"You remember the old stave, Doctor?"

The Doctor remembered no such thing. His attention was given to more substantial doctrine. "Sir, I should not be surprised if they possessed the original receipt—a local one too I am told—for dressing the red trout, in this hereditary house of entertainment."

"Never doubt it, man—claret, butter, and spiceries.—Zounds, I have eat of it till——It makes my mouth water yet. As the French adage goes,— 'Give your trout a bottle of good wine, a lump of butter, and spice, and tell me how you like him.'— Excellent trout in this very house—got in the 'Friar's cast,' man—the best reach of the river. Let them alone for that. Those jolly monks knew something of the mystery. Their warm, sunny old orchards still produce the best fruit in the country. You English gentlemen never saw the Grey-gudewife pear. Look out here, sir. The ABBOT'S HAUGH yonder—the richest carse-land and fattest beeves in the country. Their very names are genial, and smack of milk and honey!—But here comes a brother of the reformed order, whom I have never yet been able to teach the difference between Bechamel and butter-milk, though he understands ten languages. Dr. Redgill,—give me leave to present to you, my friend, Mr. Josiah Cargill, the minister of this parish. I have been telling my friend that the Reformation has thrown the science of cookery three centuries back in this corner of the island. Popery and made-dishes, Mr. Cargill,—Episcopacy, roast-bee, and plum-pudding,—and what is left to Presbytery, but its lang-kail, its brose, and mashlum bannocks?"

"So I have heard," replied Mr. Cargill; "very wholesome food, indeed."

"Wholesome food, sir! Why, your wits are wool-gathering. There is not a barefoot monk, sir, of the most beggarly, abstemious order, but can give you some pretty notions of tossing up a fricassee or an omelet, or of mixing an olio. Scotland has absolutely retrograded in gastronomy: yet she saw a better day, the memory of which is savoury in our nostrils yet, Doctor. In old Jacobite families, and in the neigh-bourhood of decayed monasteries,—in such houses as this, for instance, where long succeeding genera-tions have followed the trade of victuallers,—a few relics may still be found. It is for this reason I fix my scene of experiment at the CLEIKUM, and choose my notable hostess as high priestess of the mysteries. But here comes Mr. Winterblossom."

JEAN ANTHELME BRILLAT-SAVARIN
1755–1826

Jean Anthelme Brillat-Savarin was a lawyer and gourmet, and although he did not live to see the enormous success of his only book, *The Physiology of Taste* remains one of the most famous books on food. He came from Belley, near Lyon, growing up surrounded by the gastronomic delights of the region, before fleeing France during the Terror. For a while he worked as a violinist in New York, returning to France to become a magistrate in Paris, and was recognized as a Chevalier de l'Empire by Napoleon for his work defending Belley from the excesses of the Revolution.

He already had a reputation as a knowledgeable and able gourmet, which he cemented with food-centred gatherings at his home on the Rue Richelieu. Urged to write a book, he spent years compiling a series of essays on subjects as diverse as obesity and omelettes. However, it is his introductory aphorisms that most capture the imagination.

'Aphorisms of the Professor', from *The Physiology of Taste*

TO SERVE AS PROLEGOMENA TO HIS WORK AND ETERNAL BASIS TO THE SCIENCE.

I. The universe would be nothing were it not for life, and all that lives must be fed.

II. Animals fill themselves; man eats. The man of mind alone knows how to eat.

III. The destiny of nations depends on the manner in which they are fed.

IV. Tell me what kind of food you eat, and I will tell you what kind of man you are.

V. The Creator, when he obliges man to eat, invites him to do so by appetite, and rewards him by pleasure.

VI. *Gourmandise* is an act of our judgment, in obedience to which, we grant a preference to things which are agreeable, over those which have not that quality.

VII. The pleasure of the table belongs to all ages, to all conditions, to all countries, and to all æras; it mingles with all other pleasures, and remains at last to console us for their departure.

VIII. The table is the only place where one does not suffer from *ennui*, during the first hour.

IX. The discovery of a new dish confers more happiness on humanity, than the discovery of a new star.

X. Those persons who suffer from indigestion, or who become drunk, are utterly ignorant of the true principles of eating and drinking.

XI. The order of food is from the most substantial to the lightest.

XII. The order of drinking is from the mildest to the most foamy and perfumed.

XIII. To say that we should not change our drinks is a heresy; the tongue becomes saturated, and after the third glass yields but an obtuse sensation.

XIV. A dessert without cheese is like a beautiful woman who has lost an eye.

XV. A cook may be taught, but a man who can roast, is born with the faculty.

XVI. The most indispensable quality of a good cook is promptness. It should also be that of the guests.

XVII. To wait too long for a dilatory guest, shows disrespect to those who are punctual.

XVIII. He who receives friends and pays no attention to the repast prepared for them, is not fit to have friends.

XIX. The mistress of the house should always be certain that the coffee be excellent; the master that his *liquors* be of the first quality.

XX. To invite a person to your house is to take charge of his happiness as long as he be beneath your roof.

JEAN ANTHELME BRILLAT-SAVARIN
1755–1826

A second extract from *The Physiology of Taste*, and one which shows how Brillat-Savarin blended philosophy with tales drawn from his own experience.

As the Terror intensified in 1793, Brillat-Savarin fled to Switzerland (where he learned to make fondue), joining thousands of his fellow countrymen who found it expedient to leave. Not just aristocrats or priests (the early targets of the revolutionary mob), these were lawyers, civil servants, and the domestic staff of the upper classes. Many were chefs, who were welcomed in America and Britain. Certainly, the French diaspora helped to spread French cuisine beyond the upper echelons of English-speaking society, and by the nineteenth century the habitual disparaging of French cookery had virtually disappeared.

Here, a titled refugee in London makes his fortune by serving others, before returning to France triumphant but wise.

'Gastronomical Industry of the Émigrés', from *The Physiology of Taste*

When I was at Cologne, I found a Breton nobleman, who thought himself very fortunate, as the keeper of a public house; and I might multiply these examples indefinitely. I prefer however to tell of a Frenchman, who became very rich at London, from the skill he displayed in making salad.

He was a Limousin, and if I am not mistaken, was named Aubignac, or Albignac.

Poor as he was, he went, however, one day to dine at one of the first restaurants of London. He could always make a good dinner on a single good dish.

While he was discussing a piece of roast beef, five or six dandies sat at the next table, and one of them advanced and said, "Sir, they say your people excel in the art of making a salad. Will you be kind enough to oblige us?"

After some hesitation d'Albignac consented, and having set seriously to work, did his best.

While he was making his mixture, he replied frankly to questions about his condition, and my friend owned, not without a little blushing, that he received the aid of the English government, a circumstance which doubtless induced one of the young men to slip a ten pound bank bill into his hand.

He gave them his address, and not long after, was much surprised to receive a letter inviting him to come to dress a salad at one of the best houses in Grosvenor square.

D'Albignac began to see that he might draw considerable benefit from it, and did not hesitate to accept the offer. He took with him various preparations which he fancied would make his salad perfect as possible.

He took more pains in this second effort, and succeeded better than he had at first. On this occasion so large a sum was handed to him that he could not with justice to himself refuse to accept it.

The young men he met first, had exaggerated the salad he had prepared for them, and the second entertainment was yet louder in its praise. He became famous as "the fashionable salad-maker," and those who knew anything of satirical poetry remembered:

Désir de nonne est un feu pui dévore,
Désir d'Anglaise est cent fois piri encore.

D'Albignac, like a man of sense, took advantage of the excitement, and soon obtained a carriage, that he might travel more rapidly from one part of the town to the other. He had in a mahogany case all the ingredients he required.

Subsequently he had similar cases prepared and filled, which he used to sell by the hundred.

Ultimately he made a fortune of 80,000 francs, which he took to France when times became more peaceful.

When he had returned to France, he did not hurry to Paris, but with laudable precaution, placed 60,000 francs in the funds, and with the rest purchased a little estate, on which, for aught I know, he now lives happily. His funded money paid him fifty per cent.

These facts were imparted to me by a friend, who had known D'Albignac in London, and who had met him after his return.

WILLIAM COBBETT
1763–1835

Farmer and political activist William Cobbett first came to prominence when he launched an attack on the corruption and abuse endemic in the British armed forces. Threatened with arrest, he spent eight years in America where he became famous as 'Peter Porcupine', the name under which he wrote at the time.

Returning to Britain, he campaigned for parliamentary reform, and championed traditional agrarian society against the perceived evils of the Industrial Revolution. Increasingly depressed by the desperate poverty of the rural poor, as witnessed – and written about – in his *Rural Rides*, he came to believe that open insurrection was the only solution. This extract, from a journey undertaken in 1823, shows how dire conditions were, as the impact of the Napoleonic Wars continued to be felt, leading to starvation and terrible deprivation.

from *Rural Rides*

In quitting Sandwich, you immediately cross a river up which vessels bring coals from the sea. This marsh is about a couple of miles wide. It begins at the sea-beach, opposite the Downs, to my right hand, coming from Sandwich, and it wheels round to my left and ends at the sea-beach, opposite Margate roads. This marsh was formerly covered with the sea, very likely; and hence the land within this sort of semicircle, the name of which is Thanet, was called an *Isle*. It is, in fact, an island now, for the same reason that Portsea is an island, and that New York is an island; for there certainly is the water in this river that goes round and connects one part of the sea with the other. I had to cross this river, and to cross the marsh, before I got into the famous Isle of Thanet, which it was my intention to cross. Soon after crossing the river, I passed by a place for making salt, and could not help recollecting that there are no excisemen in these salt-making places in France, that, before the Revolution, the French were most cruelly oppressed by the duties on salt, that they had to endure, on that account, the most horrid tyranny that ever was known, except, perhaps, that practised in an *Exchequer* that shall here be nameless; that thousands and thousands of men and women were every year sent to the galleys for what was called smuggling salt; that the fathers and even the mothers were imprisoned or whipped if the children were detected in smuggling salt: I could not help reflecting, with delight, as I looked at these salt-pans in the Isle of Thanet; I could not help reflecting, that in spite of Pitt, Dundas, Perceval, and the rest of the crew, in spite of the caverns of Dover and the martello towers in Romney Marsh: in spite of all the spies and all the bayonets, and the six hundred millions of debt and the hundred and fifty millions of dead-weight, and the two hundred millions of poor-rates that are now squeezing the borough-mongers, squeezing the farmers, puzzling the fellows at Whitehall and making Mark Lane a scene of greater interest than the Chamber of the Privy Council; with delight as I jogged along under the first beams of the sun, I reflected that, in spite of all the malignant measures that had brought so much misery upon England, the gallant French people had ridded themselves of the tyranny which sent them to the galleys for endeavouring to use without tax the salt which God sent upon their shores. Can any man tell why we should still be paying five, or six, or seven shillings a bushel for salt, instead of one? We did pay fifteen shillings a bushel, tax. And why is two shillings a bushel kept on? Because, if they were taken off, the salt-tax-gathering crew must be discharged! This tax of two shillings a bushel causes the consumer to pay five, at the least, more than he would if there were no tax at all! When, great God! when shall we be allowed to enjoy God's gifts, in freedom, as the people of France enjoy them?

On the marsh I found the same sort of sheep as on Romney Marsh; but the cattle here are chiefly Welsh; black, and called runts. They are nice hardy cattle; and, I am told, that this is the description of cattle that they fat all the way up on this north side of Kent.—When I got upon the corn land in the Isle of Thanet, I got into a garden indeed. There is hardly any fallow; comparatively few turnips. It is a country of corn. Most of the harvest is in; but there are some fields of wheat and of barley not yet housed. A great many pieces of lucerne, and all of them very fine. I left Ramsgate to my right about three miles, and went right across the island to Margate; but that place is so thickly settled with stock-jobbing cuckolds, at this time of the year, that having no fancy to get their horns stuck into me, I turned away to my left when I got within about half a mile of the town. I got to a little hamlet, where I breakfasted; but could get no corn for my horse, and no bacon for myself! All was corn around me. Barns, I should think, two hundred feet long; ricks of enormous size and most numerous; crops of wheat, five quarters to an acre, on the average; and a public-house without either bacon or corn! The labourers' houses, all along through this island, beggarly in the extreme. The people dirty, poor-looking; ragged, but particularly *dirty*. The men and boys with dirty faces, and dirty smock-frocks, and dirty shirts; and, good God! what a difference between the wife of a labouring man here, and the wife of a labouring man in the forests and woodlands of Hampshire and Sussex! Invariably have I observed that the richer the soil, and the more destitute of woods; that is to say, the more purely a corn country, the more miserable the labourers. The cause is this, the great, the big bull frog grasps all. In this beautiful island every inch of land is appropriated by the rich. No hedges, no ditches, no commons, no grassy lanes: a country divided into great farms; a few trees surround the great farm-house. All the rest is bare of trees; and the wretched labourer has not a stick of wood, and has no place for a pig or cow to graze, or even to lie down upon. The rabbit countries are the countries for labouring men. There the ground is not so valuable. There it is not so easily appropriated by the few. Here, in this island, the work is almost all done by the horses. The horses plough the ground; they sow the ground; they hoe the ground; they carry the corn home; they thresh it out; and they carry it to market: nay, in this island, they *rake* the ground; they rake up the straggling straws and ears; so that they do the whole, except the reaping and the mowing. It is impossible to have an idea of anything more miserable than the state of the labourers in this part of the country.

❦
CHARLES GREVILLE
1794–1865

Were it not for his diaries, Charles Greville would
have faded into obscurity. Untitled himself, he was
nevertheless part of the aristocracy, and held various
undemanding but lucrative government positions,
well-furnished with staff to do the actual work.

From 1817, Greville kept a detailed journal, always intending it for publication. It was honest,
catty, and opinionated, and not published until after
his death. The first three volumes, heavily abridged
but nevertheless full of stories and observations
hitherto untold, caused outrage among those who
appeared within them. They remain an important
source for anyone studying the reigns of George IV,
William IV and Queen Victoria, for they do not end
until 1860 (the manuscript itself runs to twenty-nine
volumes). In this extract the extreme tedium of the
court, as well as the gaucheness of the new queen,
are laid bare.

from *The Diary of Charles Greville*

March 11th. I dined yesterday at the Palace, much to my surprise, for I had no expectation of an invitation. There was a very numerous party. We assembled in the round room next the gallery, and just before the dinner was ready the Queen entered with the Duchess of Kent, preceded by the Chamberlain [Lord Conyngham], and followed by her six ladies. She shook hands with the women, and made a sweeping bow to the men, and directly went in to dinner, conducted by Münchhausen, who sat next to her, and Lord Conyngham on the other side. The dinner was like any other great dinner. After the eating was over, the Queen's health was given by Cavendish, who sat at one end of the table, and everybody got up to drink it: a vile, vulgar custom, and, however proper it may be to drink her health elsewhere, it is bad taste to have it given by her own officer at her own table, which, in fact, is the only (private) table it is ever drunk at. However, this has been customary in the two last reigns. George III never dined but with his family, never had guests, or a dinner *party*.

The Queen sat for some time at table, talking away very merrily to her neighbours, and the men remained about a quarter of an hour after the ladies. When we went into the drawing-room, and huddled about the door in the sort of half-shy, half-awkward way people do, the Queen advanced to meet us, and spoke to everybody in succession, and if everybody's 'palaver' was as deeply interesting as mine, it would have been worth while to have had Gurney to take it down in short-hand. As the words of kings and queens are precious, and as a fair sample of a royal after-dinner colloquy, I shall record my dialogue with accurate fidelity.

Q 'Have you been riding to-day, Mr Greville?'

G 'No, Madam, I have not.'

Q 'It was a fine day.'

G 'Yes, Ma'am, a very fine day.'

Q 'It was rather cold though.'

G (*like Polonius*). 'It *was* rather cold, Madam.'

Q 'Your sister, Ly. Francis Egerton, rides I think, does not She?'

G 'She does ride sometimes, Madame.'

(A pause, when I took the lead though adhering to the same topic.)

G 'Has your Majesty been riding to-day?'

Q (*with animation*).'O yes, a very long ride.'

G 'Has your Majesty got a nice horse?'

Q 'O, a very nice horse.'

– gracious smile and inclination of head on part of Queen, profound bow on mine, and then She turned again to Lord Grey. Directly after I was (to my satisfaction) deposited at the whist table to make up the Duchess of Kent's party, and all the rest of the company were arranged about a large round table (the Queen on the sofa by it), where they passed about an hour and a half in what was probably the smallest possible talk, interrupted and enlivened, however, by some songs which Lord Ossulston sang. We had plenty of instrumental music during and after dinner. To form an opinion or the slightest notion of her real character and capacity from such a formal affair as this, is manifestly impossible Nobody expects from her any clever, amusing, or interesting talk, above all no stranger can expect it. She is very civil to everybody, and there is more of frankness, cordiality, and good-humour in her manner than of dignity. She looks and speaks cheerfully: there was nothing to criticise, nothing particularly to admire. The whole thing seemed to be dull, perhaps unavoidably so, but still so dull that it is a marvel how anybody can like such a life. This was an unusually large party, and therefore more than usually dull and formal; but it is much the same sort of thing every day. Melbourne was not there, which I regretted, as I had some curiosity to see Her Majesty and her Minister together.

❦

WILLIAM THACKERAY
1811–1863

Born in Calcutta but brought up in Britain, William Thackeray was one of Victorian Britain's best-loved novelists. He is best known for his contemporary fiction, but his journalism, essays and short stories were also well-regarded at the time. He was also an illustrator, most notably for *Punch*. He was a keen critic of social injustice and hypocrisy, especially among the upper classes in which he moved.

This extract, written under the pseudonym Michael Angelo Titmarsh, comes from one of over three hundred pieces written between 1840, when his wife suffered a total mental collapse and was permanently hospitalized, and 1847, when *Vanity Fair* started to appear. He used many different pennames and explored a number of different genres, but struggled financially until *Vanity Fair* made his name. Titmarsh was Thackeray's favourite penname, and this essay sees the writer giving a detailed critique of where to eat in Paris. It is preceded by an exhortation to English eaters to embrace variety and learn to truly love their food.

from *Memorials of Gormandising*

I simply wish to introduce to public notice a brief
dinner-journal. It has been written with the utmost
honesty and simplicity of purpose; and exhibits a
picture or table of the development of the human
mind under a series of gastronomic experiments,
diversified in their nature, and diversified, conse-
quently, in their effects. A man in London has not,
for the most part, the opportunity to make these
experiments. You are a family man, let us presume,
and you live in that metropolis for half a century. You
have on Sunday, say, a leg of mutton and potatoes
for dinner. On Monday you have cold mutton and
potatoes. On Tuesday, hashed mutton and potatoes;
the hashed mutton being flavoured with little damp
triangular pieces of toast, which always surrounded
that charming dish. Well, on Wednesday, the mutton
ended, you have beef: the beef undergoes the same
alternations of cookery, and disappears. Your life
presents a succession of joints, varied every now and
then by a bit of fish and some poultry. You drink
three glasses of a brandyfied liquor called sherry at
dinner; your excellent lady imbibes one. When she
has had her glass of port after dinner, she goes up-
stairs with the children, and you fall asleep in your
arm-chair. Some of the most pure and precious

enjoyments of life are unknown to you. You eat and drink, but you do not know the *art* of eating and drinking; nay, most probably you despise those who do. 'Give me a slice of meat,' say you, very likely, 'and a fig for your gourmands.' You fancy it is very virtuous and manly all this. Nonsense, my good sir; you are indifferent because you are ignorant, because your life is passed in a narrow circle of ideas, and because you are bigotedly blind and pompously callous to the beauties and excellences beyond you.

Sir, *respect your dinner*; idolise it, enjoy it properly. You will be by many hours in the week, many weeks in the year, and many years in your life the happier if you do.

Don't tell us that it is not worthy of a man. All a man's senses are worthy of employment, and should be cultivated as a duty. The senses are the arts. What glorious feasts does Nature prepare for your eye in animal form, in landscape, and painting! Are you to put out your eyes and not see? What royal dishes of melody does her bounty provide for you in the shape of poetry, music, whether windy or wiry, notes of the human voice, or ravishing song of birds! Are you to stuff your ears with cotton, and vow that the sense of hearing is unmanly? – you obstinate dolt you! No, surely; nor must you be so absurd as to fancy that the art of eating is in any way less worthy than the other two. You like your dinner, man; never be ashamed to say so. If you don't like your victuals, pass on to the next article; but remember that every man who has been worth a fig in this world, as poet, painter, or musician, has had a good appetite and a good taste. Ah, what a poet Byron would have been had he taken his meals properly, and allowed himself to grow fat – if nature intended him to grow fat – and not have physicked his intellect with wretched opium pills and acrid vinegar, that sent his principles to sleep, and turned his feelings sour! If that man had respected his dinner, he never would have written 'Don Juan'.

Allons donc! enough sermonising; let us sit down and fall to at once.

❦

CHARLES DICKENS
1812–1870

One of the most iconic British Victorian writers, Charles Dickens was phenomenally popular in his day and has remained so ever since. His characters blend allegory with very recognizable humanity, and many of their names have entered the English language independently of the books.

A Christmas Carol was one of a series of Dickensian Christmas books, all variations on the same theme. The 1840s was a key period for the reinvention of Christmas, transforming it from a rather riotous and plebeian festival to one which was more family oriented. Food and drink had long been a large part of the celebration, and already certain dishes – turkey, brawn, roast beef and plum pudding to name just a few – became indelibly associated with it. This extract is set on Christmas morning, as Londoners buy the last few bits for their feast.

from *A Christmas Carol*

The Ghost of Christmas Present rose.

'Spirit,' said Scrooge submissively, 'conduct me where you will. I went forth last night on compulsion, and I learnt a lesson which is working now. Tonight, if you have aught to teach me, let me profit by it.'

'Touch my robe.'

Scrooge did as he was told, and held it fast.

Holly, mistletoe, red berries, ivy, turkeys, geese, game, poultry, brawn, meat, pigs, sausages, oysters, pies, puddings, fruit, and punch, all vanished instantly. So did the room, the fire, the ruddy glow, the hour of night, and they stood in the city streets on Christmas morning, where (for the weather was severe) the people made a rough, but brisk and not unpleasant kind of music, in scraping the snow from the pavement in front of their dwellings, and from the tops of their houses, whence it was mad delight to the boys to see it come plumping down into the road below, and splitting into artificial little snowstorms.

The house fronts looked black enough, and the windows blacker, contrasting with the smooth white sheet of snow upon the roofs, and with the dirtier snow upon the ground; which last deposit had been ploughed up in deep furrows by the heavy wheels of carts and waggons; furrows that crossed and recrossed each other hundreds of times where the great streets branched off; and made intricate channels, hard to trace in the thick yellow mud and icy water. The sky was gloomy, and the shortest streets were choked up with a dingy mist, half thawed, half frozen, whose heavier particles descended in a shower of sooty atoms, as if all the chimneys in Great Britain had, by one consent, caught fire, and were blazing away to their dear hearts' content. There was nothing very cheerful in the climate or the town, and yet was there an air of cheerfulness abroad that the clearest summer air and brightest summer sun might have endeavoured to diffuse in vain.

For, the people who were shovelling away on the housetops were jovial and full of glee; calling out to one another from the parapets, and now and then exchanging a facetious snowball – better-natured missile far than many a wordy jest – laughing heartily if it went right and not less heartily if it went wrong. The poulterers' shops were still half open, and the fruiterers' were radiant in their glory. There were great, round, pot-bellied baskets of chestnuts, shaped like the waistcoats of jolly old gentlemen, lolling at the doors, and tumbling out into the street in their apoplectic opulence. There were ruddy, brown-faced, broad-girthed Spanish onions, shining in the fatness of their growth like Spanish friars, and winking from their shelves in wanton slyness at the girls as they went by, and glanced demurely at the hung-up mistletoe. There were pears and apples, clustered high in blooming pyramids; there were bunches of grapes, made, in the shopkeepers' benevolence, to dangle from conspicuous hooks, that people's mouths might water gratis as they passed; there were piles of filberts, mossy and brown, recalling, in their fragrance, ancient walks among the woods, and pleasant shufflings ankle deep through withered leaves; there were Norfolk biffins, squat and swarthy, setting off the yellow of the oranges and lemons, and, in the great compactness of their juicy persons, urgently entreating and beseeching to be carried home in paper bags and eaten after dinner. The very gold and silver fish, set forth among these choice fruits in a bowl, though members of a dull and stagnant-blooded race, appeared to know that there was something going on; and, to a fish, went gasping round and round their little world in slow and passionless excitement.

The grocers'! oh, the grocers'! nearly closed, with perhaps two shutters down, or one; but through those gaps such glimpses! It was not alone that the scales descending on the counter made a merry sound, or that the twine and roller parted company so briskly, or that the canisters were rattled up and down like juggling tricks, or even that the blended scents of tea and coffee were so grateful to the nose, or even that the raisins were so plentiful and rare, the almonds so extremely white, the sticks of cinnamon so long and straight, the other spices so delicious, the candied fruits so caked and spotted with molten sugar as to make the coldest lookers-on feel faint and subsequently bilious. Nor was it that the figs were moist and pulpy, or that the French plums blushed in modest tartness from their highly-decorated boxes, or that everything was good to eat and in its Christmas dress; but the customers were all so hurried and so eager in the hopeful promise of the day, that they tumbled up against each other at the door, crashing their wicker baskets wildly, and left their purchases upon the counter, and came running back to fetch them, and committed hundreds of the like mistakes, in the best humour possible; while the grocer and his people were so frank and fresh that the polished hearts with which they fastened their aprons behind might have been their own, worn outside for general inspection, and for Christmas daws to peck at if they chose.

But soon the steeples called good people all, to

church and chapel, and away they came, flocking through the streets in their best clothes, and with their gayest faces. And at the same time there emerged from scores of by-streets, lanes, and name-less turnings, innumerable people, carrying their dinners to the bakers' shops. The sight of these poor revellers appeared to interest the spirit very much, for he stood with Scrooge beside him in a baker's doorway, and taking off the covers as their bearers passed, sprinkled incense on their dinners from his torch. And it was a very uncommon kind of torch, for once or twice when there were angry words between some dinner-carriers who had jostled each other, he shed a few drops of water on them from it, and their good humour was restored directly. For they said, it was a shame to quarrel upon Christmas Day. And so it was. God love it, so it was.

In time the bells ceased, and the bakers' were shut up; and yet there was a genial shadowing forth of all these dinners and the progress of their cook-ing, in the thawed blotch of wet above each baker's oven; where the pavement smoked as if its stones were cooking too.

'Is there a peculiar flavour in what you sprinkle from your torch?' asked Scrooge.

'There is. My own.'

'Would it apply to any kind of dinner on this day?' asked Scrooge.

'To any kindly given. To a poor one most.'

'Why to a poor one most?' asked Scrooge.

'Because it needs it most.'

'Spirit,' said Scrooge, after a moment's thought, 'I wonder you, of all the beings in the many worlds about us, should desire to cramp these people's opportunities of innocent enjoyment.'

'I?' cried the spirit.

'You would deprive them of their means of dining every seventh day, often the only day on which they can be said to dine at all,' said Scrooge. 'Wouldn't you?'

'I?' cried the spirit.

'You seek to close these places on the seventh day,' said Scrooge. 'And it comes to the same thing!'

'I seek?' exclaimed the spirit.

'Forgive me if I am wrong. It has been done in your name, or at least in that of your family,' said Scrooge.

'There are some upon this earth of yours,' returned the spirit, 'who lay claim to know us, and who do their deeds of passion, pride, ill-will, hatred, envy, bigotry, and selfishness in our name, who are as strange to us and all our kith and kin, as if they had never lived. Remember that, and charge their doings on themselves, not us.'

WILLIAM YARRELL
1784–1856

William Yarrell was a naturalist and prolific writer, publishing on topics related to birds and fish. His *History of British Birds* was published in 3 volumes, and became the standard work for ornithologists for many decades. He was particularly keen on describing edible species, and was known for his care in consuming the specimens he collected and documented, to check that they really were good for eating.

This rather curious recipe, set out as a poem, was part of his discussion of mute swans. It was, apparently, habitually included as a printed copy with swans sent out from Norwich, the centre of the swan-breeding industry. Swans had long been popular as a feast bird, due to their size and reasonable eating, and although they were declining in popularity by the Victorian era, it was still possible to buy cygnets fattened for the table in the 1930s.

'To Roast a Swan',
from *A History of British Birds*

TO ROAST A SWAN

Take three pounds of beef, beat fine in a mortar,
Put it into the Swan—that is, when you've caught her,
Some pepper, salt, mace, some nutmeg, an onion,
Will heighten the flavour in Gourmand's opinion.
Then tie it up tight with a small piece of tape,
That the gravy and other things may not escape.
A meal paste, rather stiff, should be laid on the breast,
And some whited brown paper should cover the rest.
Fifteen minutes at least ere the Swan you take down,
Pull the paste off the bird, that the breast may get brown.

THE GRAVY.

To a gravy of beef, good and strong, I opine,
You'll be right if you add half a pint of port wine;
Pour this through the Swan, yes, quite through the belly,
Then serve the whole up with some hot currant jelly.

NB. The Swan must not be skinned.

HENRY MAYHEW
1812–1887

Failed lawyer-turned-playwright and journalist Henry Mayhew was responsible not only for one of the seminal works on the Victorian working class, but also co-founded *Punch*, one of the emblematic magazines of the era. His life was characterized by dilettantism and an inability to finish things. However, while working for the *Morning Chronicle*, he not only produced a full series of eighty-two articles, but also turned these into a work which resonated with contemporaries and was a precursor to many later studies of social inequality.

Mayhew spent two years among the street-sellers and traders of London, publishing their stories in their own voices. He became radicalized by the poverty and terrible working conditions he experienced, and for a while a labour fund flourished off the back of his articles. Obsessed with detail and statistics, his work is a vital source for the period. Reading his prose, the reader can almost taste the pea soup, and hear the cries so familiar to Londoners of the time.

'Of the Street Sellers of Hot Eels and Pea-Soup', from *London Labour and the London Poor*

Two of the condiments greatly relished by the chilled labourers and others who regale themselves on street luxuries, are "pea-soup" and "hot eels." Of these tradesmen there may be 500 now in the streets on a Saturday. As the two trades are frequently carried on by the same party, I shall treat of them together. The greatest number of these stands is in Old-street, St. Luke's, about twenty. In warm weather these street-cooks deal only in "hot eels" and whelks; as the whelk trade is sometimes an accompaniment of the others, for then the soup will not sell. These dealers are stationary, having stalls or stands in the street, and the savoury odour from them attracts more hungry-looking gazers and longers than does a cook-shop window. They seldom move about, but generally frequent the same place. A celebrated dealer of this class has a stand in Clare-street, Clare-market, opposite a cat's-meat shop; he has been heard to boast, that he wouldn't soil his hands at the business if he didn't get his 30*s*. a day, and his 2*l*. 10*s*. on a Saturday. Half this amount is considered to be about the truth. This person has mostly all the trade for hot eels in the Clare-market district. There is another "hot eel purveyor" at the end of Windmill-street, Tottenham-court-road, that does a very good trade. It is thought that he makes about 5s. a day at the business, and about 10s. on Saturday. There was, before the removals, a man who came out about five every afternoon, standing in the New-cut, nearly opposite the Victoria Theatre, his "girl" always attending to the stall. He had two or three lamps with "hot eels" painted upon them, and a handsome stall. He was considered to make about 7s. a day by the sale of eels alone, but he dealt in fried fish and pickled whelks as well, and often had a pile of fried fish a foot high. Near the Bricklayers' Arms, at the junction of the Old and New Kent-roads, a hot-eel man dispenses what a juvenile customer assured me was "as spicy as any in London, as if there was gin in it." But the dealer in Clare-market does the largest trade of all in the hot-eel line. He is "the head man." On one Saturday he was known to sell 100 lbs. of eels, and on most Saturdays he will get rid of his four "draughts" of eels (a draught being 20 lbs.) He and his son are dressed in Jenny Lind hats, bound with blue velvet, and both dispense the provisions, while the daughter attends to wash the cups. "On a Sunday, anybody," said my informant, "would think him the first nobleman or squire in the land, to see him dressed in his white hat, with black crape round it, and his drab paletot and mother-o'-pearl buttons, and black kid gloves, with the fingers too long for him."

I may add, that even the very poorest, who have only a halfpenny to spend, as well as those with better means, resort to the stylish stalls in preference to the others. The eels are all purchased at Billingsgate early in the morning. The parties themselves, or their sons or daughters, go to Billingsgate, and the watermen row them to the Dutch eel vessels moored off the market. The fare paid to the watermen is 1*d.* for every 10 lbs. purchased and brought back in the boat, the passenger being gratis. These dealers generally trade on their own capital; but when some have been having "a flare up," and have "broke down for stock," to use the words of my informant, they borrow 1*l.*, and pay it back in a week or a fortnight at the outside, and give 2*s.* for the loan of it. The money is usually borrowed of the barrow, truck, and basket-lenders. The amount of capital required for carrying on the business of course depends on the trade done; but even in a small way, the utensils cost 1*l.* They consist of one fish-kettle and one soup-kettle, holding upon an average three gallons each; besides these, five basins and five cups and ten spoons are required, also a washhand basin to wash the cups, basins, and spoons in, and a board and tressel on which the whole stand. In a large way, it requires from 3*l.* to 4*l.* to fit up a handsome stall. For this the party would have "two fine kettles," holding about four gallons each, and two patent cast-iron fireplaces (the 1*l.* outfit only admits of the bottoms of two tin saucepans being used as fireplaces, in which charcoal is always burning to keep the eels and soup hot; the whelks are always eaten cold). The crockery and spoons would be in no way superior. A small dealer requires, over and above this sum, 10*s.* to go to market with and purchase stock, and the large dealer about 30*s.* The class of persons belonging to the business have either been bred to it, or taken to it through being out of work. Some have been disabled during their work, and have resorted to it to save themselves from the workhouse. The price of the hot eels is a halfpenny for five or seven pieces of fish, and three-parts of a cupful of liquor. The charge for a half-pint of pea-soup is a halfpenny, and the whelks are sold, according to the size, from a halfpenny each to three or four for the same sum. These are put out in saucers.

The eels are Dutch, and are cleaned and washed, and cut in small pieces of from a half to an inch each. (The daughter of one of my informants was busily engaged, as I derived this information, in the cutting of the fish. She worked at a blood-stained board, with a pile of pieces on one side and a heap of entrails on the other.) The portions so cut are then boiled, and the liquor is thickened with flour and flavoured with chopped parsley and mixed spices. It is kept hot in the streets, and served out, as I have stated, in halfpenny cupfuls, with a small quantity of vinegar and pepper. The best purveyors add a little butter. The street-boys are extravagant in their use of vinegar.

To dress a draught of eels takes three hours—to clean, cut them up, and cook them sufficiently; and the cost is now 5s. 2d. (much lower in the summer) for the draught (the 2d. being the expense of "shoring"), 8d. for 4 lb. of flour to thicken the liquor, 2d. for the parsley to flavour it, and 1s. 6d. for the vinegar, spices, and pepper (about three quarts of vinegar and two ounces of pepper). This quantity, when dressed and seasoned, will fetch in halfpenny-worths from 15s. to 18s. The profit upon this would be from 7s. to 9s. 6d.; but the cost of the charcoal has to be deducted, as well as the salt used while cooking. These two items amount to about 5d.

The pea-soup consists of split peas, celery, and beef bones. Five pints, at 3-1/2d. a quart, are used to every three gallons; the bones cost 2d., carrots 1d., and celery 1/2d.—these cost 1s. 0-1/4d.; and the pepper, salt, and mint, to season it, about 2d. This, when served in halfpenny basinfuls, will fetch from

2s. 3d. to 2s. 4d., leaving 1s. 1d. profit. But from this the expenses of cooking must be taken; so that the clear gain upon three gallons comes to about 11d. In a large trade, three kettles, or twelve gallons, of pea-soup will be disposed of in the day, and about four draughts, or 80 lbs., of hot eels on every day but Saturday,—when the quantity of eels disposed of would be about five draughts, or 100 lbs. weight, and about 15 gallons of pea-soup. Hence the profits of a good business in the hot-eel and pea-soup line united will be from 7l. to 7l. 10s. per week, or more. But there is only one man in London does this amount of business, or rather makes this amount of money. A small business will do about 15 lbs. of eels in the week, including Saturday, and about 12 gallons of soup. Sometimes credit is given for a half-pennyworth, or a pennyworth, at the outside; but very little is lost from bad debts. Boys who are partaking of the articles will occasionally say to the proprietor of the stall, "Well, master, they are nice; trust us another ha'p'orth, and I'll pay you when I comes again;" but they are seldom credited, for the stall-keepers know well they would never see them again. Very often the stock cooked is not disposed of, and then it is brought home and eaten by the family. The pea-soup will seldom keep a night, but what is left the family generally use for supper.

The dealers go out about half-past ten in the morning, and remain out till about ten at night. Monday is the next best day to Saturday. The generality of the customers are boys from 12 to 16 years of age. Newsboys are very partial to hot eels—women prefer the pea-soup. Some of the boys will have as many as six halfpenny cupfuls consecutively on a Saturday night; and some women will have three halfpenny basinsful of soup. Many persons in the cold weather prefer the hot soup to beer. On wet, raw, chilly days, the soup goes off better than usual, and in fine weather there is a greater demand for the hot eels. One dealer assured me that he once *did* serve two gentlemen's servants with twenty-eight halfpenny cupfuls of hot eels one after another. One servant had sixteen, and the other twelve cupfuls, which they ate all at one standing; and one of these customers was so partial to hot eels, that he used to come twice a day every day for six months after that, and have eight cupfuls each day, four at noon and four in the evening. These two persons were the best customers my informant ever had. Servants, however, are not generally partial to the commodity. Hot eels are not usually taken for dinner, nor is pea-soup, but throughout the whole day, and just at the fancy of the passers-by. There are no shops for the sale of these articles. The dealers keep no accounts of what their receipts and expenditure are.

The best time of the year for the hot eels is from the middle of June to the end of August. On some days during that time a person in a small way of business will clear upon an average 1s. 6d. a day, on other days 1s.; on some days, during the month of August, as much as 2s. 6d. a day. Some cry out "Nice hot eels—nice hot eels!" or "Warm your hands and fill your bellies for a halfpenny." One man used to give his surplus eels, when he considered his sale completed on a night, to the poor creatures refused admission into a workhouse, lending them his charcoal fire for warmth, which was always returned to him. The poor creatures begged cinders, and carried the fire under a railway arch. The general rule, however, is for the dealer to be silent, and merely expose the articles for sale. "I likes better," said one man to me, "to touch up people's noses than their heyes or their hears." There are now in the trade almost more than can get a living at it, and their earnings are less than they were formerly. One party attributed this to the opening of a couple of penny-pie shops in his neighborhood. Before then he could get 2s. 6d. a day clear, take one day with another; but since the establishment of the business in the penny-pie line he cannot take above 1s. 6d. a day clear. On the day the first of these pie-shops opened, it made as much as 10 lbs., or half a draught of eels, difference to him There was a band of music and an illumination at the pie-shop, and it was impossible to stand against that. The fashionable dress of the trade is the "Jenny Lind" or "wide-awake" hat, with a broad black ribbon tied round it, and a white apron and sleeves. The dealers usually go to Hampton-court or Greenwich on a fine Sunday. They are partial to the pit of Astley's. One of them told his waterman at Billingsgate the other morning that "he and his good lady had been werry amused with the osses at Hashley's last night."

ELIZA ACTON
1799–1859

Eliza Acton worked as a teacher and poet before writing, at the behest of her publishers, 'something practical'. She published *Modern Cookery for Private Families* in 1845 and it remains one of the finest recipe books published in English. It was immensely influential, for it had a clarity and exactness rare in books of the time. She followed this up with the *English Bread Book*, which was part recipe book, part polemic, together with a detailed examination of the conditions under which bread was produced.

This extract explains her approach in typically down-to-earth prose. Later she goes on to explore the insanitary and miserable conditions of Victorian bakers, who often worked throughout the night in dank, rat-infested cellars, locked in by unscrupulous master-bakers. Consumers refused to pay more for their bread, and corners were inevitably cut. Analysis of bread in London in the 1850s revealed that not one loaf was unadulterated, be it with alum, plaster of Paris or simply inferior ground grains.

The bread question, in all its bearings, appears to have excited a far more earnest degree of interest in France, Belgium, and some parts of Germany, up to the present moment, than with us; and the practical results of it in those countries have been highly satisfactory and beneficial.

A general impression seems to exist there, amongst the intelligent orders of society, of the absolute necessity of a *thorough reform* in the old methods of "panification," or bread-making; some not very attractive pictures of which are given in several of their recent publications on the subject, written by men of ability, who have entered with great zeal into the subject. They all concur in stating, that for centuries past there has been no real improvement in the operations of the baking-trade; and that while striking and rapid progress has been made in all other of the industrial arts, these—faulty as they are—have remained unaltered. The insalubrity, coarseness, and want of economy, which distinguish them are thus described, and commented on, in the archives of the French *Académie des Sciences*, and in various expositions which have been made through the press, or at the meetings of learned societies. I insert some of the details—unattractive as they are—without softening them for the fastidious reader, because any disgust which they may inspire, will be a natural and healthy consequence, and may awaken a desire to aid in their abolishment. It is not well to shut our eyes, and determine to ask and to see nothing of evils which more or less affect life itself; though thousands of irreflective persons prefer to do this, rather than to investigate and endeavour to remove them. Many do not even *choose to believe* that the water supplied to the inhabitants of London requires purifying before it can be drunk with safety; or that the imperfect sewerage of that mighty city, so taints and loads the air with disease, as to render it often a deadly poison to those who inhale it. So it is with regard to the bread they eat. They do not wish to be disturbed in their belief that it is all that it ought to be; and treat as pure fancy, or prejudice, the idea that it *can* disagree with anybody, or be productive of serious and painful disorders. The common mode of making it is too well known to admit of contradiction. It is thus not very invitingly described by a foreign contemporary:—"It will be asked by our descendants, with astonishment, if indeed it could be true that, at this epoch of industrial progress, our principal aliment were prepared in the gross manner that it is, by plunging the arms into the dough, and raising and tossing it about with such force as to exhaust the strength of the half-naked journeymen, and cause streams of perspiration to flow and mingle with the alimentary substance?"

And again:—

"If instead of being satisfied with the aspect of the loaves exhibited in the windows of the bakers' shops, we were to descend into the offices where they are made, and witness the want of cleanliness and wholesomeness which attend their fabrication; could see *here* a reservoir of water *which is never changed; there* supplies of flour exposed to the influence of an impure atmosphere, either too damp or over-heated; and above all, sickly, perspiring men in contact with our food, we should turn away with a very legitimate feeling of disgust."

These are revolting pictures, but they are true; yet much which repels us in them is beyond the control of the bakers themselves, arising from the want of space, and fitting accommodation for the trade they follow. How can the air of the ill-ventilated underground premises in which their operations are carried on generally in populous and crowded cities, be otherwise than most unhealthily foul, destructive to the men employed in them, and having the worst effects on the food which they prepare? No article of our nourishment requires more scrupulous nicety in everything connected with its fabrication than bread.

Its value—which cannot well be over-estimated—is *dependent on its purity*; and this can be preserved (even when it is composed of *genuine* ingredients) only by the utmost *cleanliness* in all the details of its preparation, and the absence of every unwholesome influence in the locality where it is effected.

ALEXIS SOYER
1810–1858

Possibly the first true celebrity in the British culinary world, Alexis Soyer was a French émigré who trained in restaurants and private establishments before leaving the country after the second French Revolution of 1830. In England, he quickly rose to fame as the chef at the Reform Club, where he installed a new kitchen, complete with gas for cooking, and was tireless in inventing new dishes. As his reputation increased and he threw himself into work after the death of his wife, Emma, his culinary adventures became ever more impressive.

Culinary Campaign was one of many books authored by Soyer, though most were recipe books. It narrates his time in the Crimea, where he went, without pay, to reorganize the catering at the military hospitals. The field stoves he devised for use became standard equipment for the British army until well into the twentieth century. This extract tells of the terrible conditions he encountered, one among many reasons the death toll from disease was so high.

from *Culinary Campaign*

Having called upon Doctor Taylor, I had a long conversation with him upon cookery. In the course of this he said,—

"On finding that the cooking was so badly done, I took upon myself, not only to superintend the men, but also to cook and teach them; and I must say I found them very willing. How could I expect them to know anything about it? they had never been taught to do it."

"True, Doctor; and, as soon as they begin to know a little about it, they are recalled to their regiments, and replaced by new-comers as ignorant as they were themselves at first."

"Exactly; and I tell you what, Monsieur Soyer, though we may be very good doctors, and possess a thorough knowledge of medical science, we still need the aid of culinary science; for the one without the other will produce but very unsatisfactory results. Since I have turned my attention to it, I am more and more fortified in the opinion which I have expressed before several medical boards, that a doctor, to be well qualified, should have some knowledge of the art of cookery, and this he ought to acquire in the first stage of his medical education."

"Indeed, Doctor, it is not with the view of elevating

my profession, to which I have now devoted my attention for more than twenty-seven years, that I say I am persuaded that this science has been too lightly treated. In corroboration of your just remark, I have, as you will find, already stated in my various works upon cookery, that to make a good cook it is of paramount importance that a man should possess some chemical as well as medical knowledge."

"I agree with you, Monsieur Soyer," said he.

"As soon as my kitchen is ready, Doctor, I hope you will favour me with a visit."

"With much pleasure. Let me know when it is finished."

To my great regret, I was obliged to see about returning to Pera, some delay having taken place in the completion of my house. On reaching the landing-place not a caique was to be had, the weather was so bad they could not cross. A friend offered me shelter for that night at a small restaurant kept by a Greek called Demetri. There were seventeen of us lying on straw sofas, with the privilege of covering ourselves with our great coats, if fortunate enough to possess one. Rooms were at a premium in Scutari. It was also necessary for anybody who wished to have the benefit of his great-coat to keep awake all night; for no sooner did you begin to doze than some of your sleeping partners, who happened to be wide awake, endeavoured to appropriate the coveted garment to their use; and the weather being very chilly, this proved anything but pleasant. Unfortunately, after passing an uncomfortable night, I did not feel much refreshed, and was almost unfit to undertake the difficult task I had before me. However, I was up at six, and in the kitchen by seven. None of my orders had been attended to. My own people were not there as they ought to have been; and the men told me they could not get the rations till ten o'clock, that being the usual time for issuing them.

"Really," said I; "and pray who told you so?"

"The serjeant and some of the orderlies," was the reply.

"We shall see all about that; come with me."

The truth is, I did find it very difficult to get anything; but, in less than half-an-hour after I had been to the purveyor's head-quarters my new regiment began to manœuvre admirably under my command. By eight o'clock everything was ready for the cooking, except my cooks, who had been sleeping in a store-room upon some straw, and had a regular fray with the allied rats. These animals, it appears, had come to welcome them to Scutari.

Upon inspecting the boilers, my first fear was realized—there was nothing but copper—all the tinning had worn away. And very difficult was it to ascertain this fact, these immense and deep caldrons being securely screwed to the marble basement, and extremely difficult, not only to remove, but also to tin when removed. I consider it most advisable that all large establishments should have their cooking apparatus made of malleable iron, which is extremely clean, is much cheaper, and does not require tinning: the lid may be made of copper for appearance' sake, but not so the boiler. The kitchen battery of the wealthy alone should be copper, as they can afford to employ professional persons for the preparation of their diet, who never would attempt using them when coppery.

That day I was obliged to use them. Having put the proper quantity of water into each copper, with the meat, barley, vegetables, and salt and pepper, we lighted the fires; and after allowing the ingredients to simmer for two hours and a half, an excellent soup was made; I only adding a little sugar and flour to finish it.

The receipt for this excellent soup, so highly approved of and immediately adopted by the medical men, will be found in my Hospital Diets, with a scale of proportions from ten to a hundred.

The meat was so poor that there was no fat to skim off the soup. It was therefore served out at once, as described in the receipt. Several doctors went round with me, and asked the men how they liked it. They were all highly delighted with it, and praised it very much. I also took care that the rations of meat should not be tied together on the skewer.

The orderlies were now ordered not to tie their rations of meat so tight. Upon inspection I found that they had a most curious method of marking their different lots. Some used a piece of red cloth cut from an old jacket; others half a dozen old buttons tied together; old knives, forks, scissors, &c., but one in particular had hit upon an idea which could not fail to meet with our entire approval. The discovery of this brilliant idea was greeted with shouts of laughter from Miss Nightingale, the doctors, and myself. It consisted in tying a pair of old snuffers to the lot.

All this rubbish was daily boiled with the meat, but probably required more cooking. On telling the man with the snuffers that it was a very dirty trick to put such things in the soup, the reply was—"How can it be dirty, sir? sure they have been boiling this last month."

When all the dinners had been served out, I perceived a large copper half full of rich broth with about three inches of fat upon it. I inquired what they did with this?

"Throw it away, sir."

"Throw it away?" we all exclaimed.

"Yes, sir; it's the water in which the fresh beef has been cooked."

"Do you call that water? I call it strong broth. Why don't you make soup of it?"

"We orderlies don't like soup, sir."

"Then you really do throw it away?"

"Yes, sir; it is good for nothing."

I took a ladle and removed a large basinful of beautiful fat, which, when cold, was better for cooking purposes than the rank butter procured from Constantinople at from ten to fifteen piastres per pound. The next day I showed the men how to make a most delicious soup with what they had before so foolishly thrown away. This method they were henceforward very glad to adopt. Not less than seventy pounds of beef had been daily boiled in this manner, and without salt. It would hardly be credited, but for its truth I can appeal to Miss Nightingale and others who were present.

Nothing was needed but a sharp look-out after the cooks in order to ensure complete success. The day after I had the coppers tinned. The next thing was to have a charcoal stove built, an oven, a storeroom, and a larder partitioned off; and a kitchen dresser and chopping-block made. Through the kindness of the Chief Engineer, Captain Gordon these things were accomplished in a few days, and a a trifling expense. If not a very magnificent, it was as will be seen, a very spacious and handy kitchen.

In a few days I made experiments in small quantities upon all the various extra diets, such as chicken, mutton, and veal broth, the cooking of fowls, beef and mutton tea, &c. I did not forget the beverages, such as rice water, lemonades, arrow-root, panada ditto, barley water, sago jelly, &c.; rice pudding, sago, bread, vermicelli and macaroni ditto.

A gentleman, Mr. Black, who was a first-class interpreter, was then introduced to me by the Purveyor-in-Chief, and appointed to assist me in any way I might require his aid. He was highly recommended by Miss Nightingale, and a number of first-class doctors, as well as by Lord William Paulet. It is with gratitude that I acknowledge the great assistance I received from that gentleman during his stay with me, and the energy he displayed in procuring everything I required. He spoke French fluently, also the Turkish, Greek, and American languages. This rendered him invaluable to me, as I was obliged to employ people speaking those different languages in my numerous kitchens. And what was more remarkable still, he was the husband of the celebrated Maid of Athens, whose company I had the pleasure of enjoying several times; and although this interesting personage is now in her tenth lustre, some remains of the eulogy of the great Byron seem still engraved on the physiognomy of the once cele-brated Greek beauty; and she informed me that when Lord Byron wrote his poem on her, she was but ten years of age, he at the time residing opposite the house of her parents at Athens.

OWEN MEREDITH
1831–1891

Owen Meredith was the pen name of Edward Robert Bulwer-Lytton, the first earl of Lytton. He was a career diplomat as well as a poet, working in the US as well as across Europe before becoming Viceroy of India in 1876. *Lucile*, which was his best-received work, was a novel set in the form of verse, intended to echo continental writing in a similar vein.

This extract tells the story of Lucile's love rivals, and then of their children. In this scene, one of the two contenders for Lucile is distracted from his passion by the very important occasion of dinner. The second stanza still resonates today.

'Lucile'

XVIII.

O hour of all hours, the most bless'd upon earth,
Blesséd hour of our dinners!

                          The land of his birth;
The face of his first love; the bills that he owes;
The twaddle of friends and the venom of foes;
The sermon he heard when to church he last went;
The money he borrow'd, the money he spent; —
All of these things a man, I believe, may forget,
And not be the worse for forgetting; but yet
Never, never, oh never! earth's luckiest sinner
Hath unpunish'd forgotten the hour of his dinner!
Indigestion, that conscience of every bad stomach,
Shall relentlessly gnaw and pursue him with some ache
Or some pain; and trouble, remorseless, his best case,
As the Furies once troubled the sleep of Orestes.

XIX.

We may live without poetry, music, and art;
We may live without conscience, and live without heart;
We may live without friends; we may live without books;
But civilized man cannot live without cooks.

He may live without books, — what is knowledge but
    grieving?
He may live without hope, — what is hope but deceiving?
He may live without love, — what is passion but pining?
But where is the man that can live without dining?

CHARLES SELBY
1802–1863

Charles Selby (real name George Wilson) was an actor and playwright who had a reasonable reputation as a character actor and writer of farce. He also used alter egos, who he portrayed both on the stage and used as pseudonyms for comic journalism and short skits. One of these was Tabitha Tickletooth, and Selby is resplendent in full costume as he gazes from the front cover of the book he authored under her name.

Despite being a comic book, Selby's (or Tickletooth's) recipes are pretty sound. He prefaces them with introductory prose, and peppers the book with interludes which are as revealing of the attitudes of the middle classes at the time as they are often genuinely good pieces of advice. This extract is both cringingly horrible and also slyly pokes fun at the snobbishness it purports to reveal. It is also a useful glimpse into lower-middle-class dinners.

'English Dinner for Snobs',
from *The Dinner Question*

To the Editor of Punch.

"SIR,—Since sending to the *Times* my letter, of a column and a half in length, in which I laid down the true principles on which dinners should be given (or rather exchanged, for I need not say that a dinner creates a debt, due from those we invite, except where a writer, buffoon, traveller, or other attraction is introduced as part of the *menu*, and, indeed, he ought to be written down in it), I have been reminded that there are a good many persons in this country who, though neither millionaires, nor even possessing a decent income of three or four thousand a year, arrogate to themselves, in this levelling age, the right to know what they are eating and drinking, and who complain of the present system of dinner-giving. I allude to those whom, without my being unnecessarily offensive, I may call Snobs, with perhaps six, seven, or eight hundred a year. I have been asked to give, for the benefit of such persons, a few hints in the spirit of the letter which I addressed to their betters. It is, I fear, almost insulting their wretchedness to advise them on such a subject, but it is our duty to help our inferiors, and endeavour to make them feel that the state of life in which Providence has placed them, to labour, and look up to us for direction, is as comfortable as they deserve it should be.

"Of course, I do not speak to them of 'dinner at 8,' when, if they have worked as they ought to do, they are yawning for bed; of chairs with 'spring seats and spring backs;' of 'Sèvres china,' 'abundance of flowers,' 'child with *corbeille* full of grapes,' 'French painted moss,' 'a rose or bunch of violets by the napkin,' 'ortolans and beccaficos,' or the other necessaries of civilized life. To mock the needy is the basest vulgarity. I will merely give the Snobs I have referred to a little counsel, derived from practical knowledge of their habits and wants.

"Addressing such persons, I would say,—

"You had better give no dinners at all. It is for your betters to dine; you have only to eat. Tea, at five o'clock, with plenty of muffins, Sarah Lunnes, and toast, is a more befitting repast for you to offer to your friends: and perhaps some bread and cheese, spring onions, or even a salad, afterwards, may not be regarded as extravagance. Beer is not an unwholesome drink for the inferior classes. I suppose that your females tolerate tobacco. Why not be content with the enjoyments natural to your order?

"But, if you *will* imitate your superiors, and

ask persons to dinner, attend to the following hints:—

"Always invite the wives of your male friends. These women will much abridge the evening, being desirous to get home to their children (for whom, of course, they have no nursery governesses and nurses), and they will in some measure check intemperate habits.

"Give your meal at 6, as persons of your class are unaccustomed to wait so long, and will have lunched, whereby you will save.

"Make your table pretty, by all means. A plaster cast of the Emperor Napoleon, or a Church with coloured windows, for illumination, can be bought for a few pence; and will lead the conversation to politics, or to religion, and kindred subjects on which your class imagines itself to have a right to speak.

"To have a *menu* would be a mockery, but as you, as well as we, have 'stupid or silent guests,' let your little boys write out on copy-book paper a few maxims, and lay a copy by each person. 'Gluttony leads to want,' 'Temperance profiteth much,' 'Let not your Eye be bigger than your bell-Eye,' and similar morals, may do good, besides improving your brats' writing. Instead of a rose or violet, place by each male person a cold saveloy, and by each female a piece of gingerbread, to be 'munched' instead of bread (as in high life) during the pauses.

"Never put tallow candles on the table. A lamp is cheap, and if the mistress of the house cleans it herself, will long keep in order.

"No soup that you can make is fit to eat. But oysters may begin your dinners as well as ours, only instead of 'four or six,' let each person have a couple of dozen, with roll, butter, and beer. This will materially help you with the rest of the dinner.

"There is no objection to cheap fish, and I have seen apparently good fish cried in the streets in which you reside. But a few fresh herrings, or sprats, will be the safest. Remember that fish should be eaten with the fork, even though made of steel. But albata is not dear, and looks nice, if the mistress herself rubs it with wash-leather.

"Instead of the huge, tough, gory joints in which you delight, try hashed mutton, Irish stew, or harico. Fried potatoes are a delicacy easily attainable. The mashed potato, with small sausage on the top, will wean many a husband—not from his club, for you have, happily for you, no such temptations—but from the chop-house. Marrowbones, when you wish to be particularly 'genteel' (as you call it), may be introduced.

"Why have a pudding course? Ugly, sloppy, or

hard, unwholesome things are your puddings. G[o to]
a respectable grocer's, and ask him for an a[rticle]
called macaroni. He will tell you how to co[ok it.]
With a little grated cheese, you will find it a [great]
luxury. Treacle on toast will please the juvenil[es.]

"Then your slatternly servant (by the way [insist]
on her washing her face, and wearing a cap—never
let her come in with her bonnet on) will heave on to
the groaning table a hemicycle of cheese like half
a millstone. Keep this away, and have some slices
handed round. Do not, from a foolish feeling of
'gentility,' deny yourselves onions, which you like.
You will not be a bit more like us if you never touch
another onion to your lives' end.

"By all means have what you consider dessert.
Apples, oranges, and biscuits you have in your gallery at the theatre, why not on table? A drum of figs,
covered by one of your girls with coloured paper, or
stuck over with red wafers, will be a tasteful centre
ornament, and to the sweet fig you may charge the
bad taste of your wine. For I suppose you will give
three-and-sixpence, or even four shillings, for this
nastiness, though I advise (and your females prefer)
brandy and water.

"I tell you frankly not to be ashamed of tobacco-
pipes. We take a cigarette, and what is that but a
tobacco-pipe of paper?

143

"Your best *chasse* is being driven up-stairs to tea. The sooner this is announced the better for the temper of your females, and for your own heads when you go to your work next morning.

"Keep your children up. If they are tired and cross, it is only once in a way. They materially help to break up a party, and my object has been to show you how, with your narrow means, you may in a humble and cheerful way, imitate your superiors, while exercising a wise economy. Let me add, never hesitate, if it be a wet night, to send your maid for cabs, instead of asking your guests to delay their departure. But give the poor girl one glass of spirits; remember what you save by dismissing your friends.

"If these hints are of any use to persons with not more than eight hundred a year, I shall have done my duty to the poor, and remain,

"Your obedient servant,
"Berkeley-street.   G. H. M."

❦

ISABELLA BEETON
1836–1865

Probably the best-known British historic cookery writer, Isabella Beeton was a journalist, magazine editor and fashion writer, working as part of her husband's mini-publishing empire. In 1859 her *Book of Cookery and Household Management* started to be serialized, before being published as a full work in 1861.

The *Book of Household Management* was an instant and long-lasting bestseller, mainly as a result of canny marketing rather than the contents. Although Beeton's authorial voice was strong, and the book well-organized and clear, with heaps of additional information and facts about the sex life of fish (for example), the recipes were almost all plagiarized, frequently from Eliza Acton, and sometimes garbled.

One of the few original recipes seems to be this, the first recorded use of the term Victoria Sandwich, named for the queen. It was not until the twentieth century that Victoria lent her name to the sponge itself. It is also amazingly foolproof.

'Victoria Sandwiches',
from *Book of Household Management*

INGREDIENTS.—4 eggs; their weight in pounded sugar, butter, and flour; ¼ saltspoonful of salt, a layer of any kind of jam or marmalade.

Mode.—Beat the butter to a cream; dredge in the flour and pounded sugar; stir these ingredients well together, and add the eggs, which should be previously thoroughly whisked. When the mixture has been well beaten for about 10 minutes, butter a Yorkshire-pudding tin, pour in the batter, and bake it in a moderate oven for 20 minutes. Let it cool, spread one half of the cake with a layer of nice preserve, place over it the other half of the cake, press the pieces slightly together, and then cut it into long finger-pieces; pile them in cross-bars on a glass dish, and serve.

Time.—20 minutes. *Average cost,* 1s. 3d.

Sufficient for 5 or 6 persons. *Seasonable* at any time.

MARY ELIZABETH BRADDON
1835–1915

One of the most prolific writers of the late nineteenth century, Mary Elizabeth Braddon specialized in sensation fiction. Her book *Lady Audley's Secret* followed years of writing crime stories for the penny dreadfuls, and it both shocked and excited its readership. It, and the follow up, *Aurora Floyd*, contained bigamy, violence and very strong female heroines. She later went on to write a wide variety of thrilling novels (and some not so thrilling). Some were essentially domestic, others far less so, though all relied on the juxtaposition of domestic detail with more dangerous events.

In this extract the ethereal Lady Audley is making tea. Tea had been inextricably linked with femininity, since its introduction in the mid-seventeenth century. The scene appears to adhere to this trope, but it is unsettling – Lady Audley's portrayal here hints at darker currents beneath. These will become more apparent as the plot progresses, climaxing in arson, murder and the unmasking of a fiendishly driven villain.

from *Lady Audley's Secret*

Robert shook hands with the surgeon and returned to his uncle's room. He had been away about a quarter of an hour. Sir Michael had fallen asleep once more, and my lady's loving hands had lowered the heavy curtains and shaded the lamp by the bedside. Alicia and her father's wife were taking tea in Lady Audley's boudoir, the room next to the antechamber in which Robert and Mr Dawson had been seated.

Lucy Audley looked up from her occupation amongst the fragile china cups, and watched Robert rather anxiously, as he walked softly to his uncle's room, and back again to the boudoir. She looked very pretty and innocent, seated behind the graceful group of delicate opal china and glittering silver. Surely a pretty woman never looks prettier than when making tea. The most feminine and most domestic of all occupations imparts a magic harmony to her every movement, a witchery to her every glance. The floating mists from the boiling liquid in which she infuses the soothing herbs, whose secrets are known to her alone, envelop her in a cloud of scented vapour, through which she seems a social fairy, weaving potent spells with Gunpowder and Bohea. At the tea-table she reigns omnipotent, unapproachable. What do men know of the mysterious beverage? Read how poor Hazlitt made his tea, and shudder at the dreadful barbarism. How clumsily the wretched creatures attempt to assist the witch president of the tea-tray; how hopelessly they hold the kettle, how continually they imperil the frail cups and saucers, or the taper hands of the priestess. To do away with the tea-table is to rob woman of her legitimate empire. To send a couple of hulking men about amongst your visitors, distributing a mixture made in the housekeeper's room, is to reduce the most social and friendly of ceremonies to a formal giving out of rations. Better the pretty influence of the teacups and saucers gracefully wielded in a woman's hand, than all the inappropriate power snatched at the point of the pen from the unwilling sterner sex. Imagine all the women of England elevated to the high level of masculine intellectuality; superior to crinoline; above pearl powder and Mrs Rachel Levison; above taking the pains to be pretty; above making themselves agreeable; above tea-tables, and that cruelly scandalous and rather satirical gossip which even strong men delight in; and what a dreary, utilitarian, ugly life the sterner sex must lead.

My lady was by no means strong-minded. The starry diamond upon her white fingers flashed hither

and thither amongst the tea things, and she bent her
pretty head over the marvellous Indian tea-caddy of
sandalwood and silver, with as much earnestness as
if life held no higher purpose than the infusion of
Bohea.

'You'll take a cup of tea with us, Mr Audley?' she
asked, pausing with the teapot in her hand to look
up at Robert, who was standing near the door.

'If you please.'

'But you have not dined, perhaps? Shall I ring
and tell them to bring you something a little more
substantial than biscuits and transparent bread and
butter?'

'No, thank you, Lady Audley. I took some lunch
before I left town. I'll trouble you for nothing but a
cup of tea.'

LEWIS CARROLL
1832–1898

A mathematician, Oxford don, photographer and cleric, Lewis Carroll (Charles Dodgson) is best known for his children's books, most notably *Alice in Wonderland* and its sequel, *Through the Looking-Glass*. The character of Alice was based on a child of a friend, Alice Liddell, though an unidentified quarrel between Carroll and the Liddells saw them largely estranged by the time the book was published.

Carroll used food in several scenes, usually subverting it as he did so many aspects of life in Wonderland. The mock turtle, for example, was a riff on a popular soup made from a calf's head (hence the body of a turtle and the head of a calf). The delightfully bonkers tea party in this extract plays on notions of politeness and convention, framed within something so quotidian – yet important to get to grips with – that toy tea sets were a common part of a child's playroom.

from *Alice in Wonderland*

There was a table set out under a tree in front of the house, and the March Hare and the Hatter were having tea at it: a Dormouse was sitting between them, fast asleep, and the other two were using it as a cushion, resting their elbows on it, and talking over its head. 'Very uncomfortable for the Dormouse,' thought Alice; 'only, as it's asleep, I suppose it doesn't mind.'

The table was a large one, but the three were all crowded together at one corner of it. 'No room! No room!' they cried out when they saw Alice coming. 'There's *plenty* of room!' said Alice indignantly, and she sat down in a large armchair at one end of the table.

'Have some wine,' the March Hare said in an encouraging tone.

Alice looked all round the table, but there was nothing on it but tea. 'I don't see any wine,' she remarked.

'There isn't any,' said the March Hare.

'Then it wasn't very civil of you to offer it,' said Alice angrily.

'It wasn't very civil of you to sit down without being invited,' said the March Hare.

'I didn't know it was *your* table,' said Alice; 'it's laid for a great many more than three.'

'Your hair wants cutting,' said the Hatter. He had been looking at Alice for some time with great curiosity, and this was his first speech.

'You should learn not to make personal remarks,' Alice said with some severity: 'it's very rude.'

The Hatter opened his eyes very wide on hearing this; but all he *said* was, 'Why is a raven like a writing-desk?'

'Come, we shall have some fun now!' thought Alice. 'I'm glad they've begun asking riddles – I believe I can guess that,' she added aloud.

'Do you mean that you think you can find out the answer to it?' said the March Hare.

'Exactly so,' said Alice.

'Then you should say what you mean,' the March Hare went on.

'I do,' Alice hastily replied; 'at least – at least I mean what I say – that's the same thing, you know.'

'Not the same thing a bit!' said the Hatter. 'You might just as well say that "I see what I eat" is the same thing as "I eat what I see"!'

'You might just as well say,' added the March Hare, 'that "I like what I get" is the same thing as "I get what I like"!'

'You might just as well say,' added the Dormouse,

who seemed to be talking in his sleep, 'that "I breathe when I sleep" is the same thing as "I sleep when I breathe"!'

'It *is* the same thing with you,' said the Hatter, and here the conversation dropped, and the party sat silent for a minute, while Alice thought over all she could remember about ravens and writing-desks, which wasn't much.

The Hatter was the first to break the silence. 'What day of the month is it?' he said, turning to Alice; he had taken his watch out of his pocket, and was looking at it uneasily, shaking it every now and then, and holding it to his ear.

Alice considered a little, and then said, 'The fourth.'

'Two days wrong!' sighed the Hatter. 'I told you butter wouldn't suit the works!' he added looking angrily at the March Hare.

'It was the *best* butter,' the March Hare meekly replied.

'Yes, but some crumbs must have got in as well,' the Hatter grumbled: 'you shouldn't have put it in with the bread-knife.'

The March Hare took the watch and looked at it gloomily: then he dipped it into his cup of tea, and looked at it again: but he could think of nothing better to say than his first remark, 'It was the *best* butter, you know.'

Alice had been looking over his shoulder with some curiosity. 'What a funny watch!' she remarked. 'It tells the day of the month, and doesn't tell what o'clock it is!'

'Why should it?' muttered the Hatter. 'Does *your* watch tell you what year it is?'

'Of course not,' Alice replied very readily: 'but that's because it stays the same year for such a long time together.'

'Which is just the case with *mine*,' said the Hatter.

Alice felt dreadfully puzzled. The Hatter's remark seemed to have no sort of meaning in it, and yet it was certainly English. 'I don't quite understand you,' she said, as politely as she could.

'The Dormouse is asleep again,' said the Hatter, and he poured a little hot tea upon its nose.

The Dormouse shook its head impatiently, and said, without opening its eyes, 'Of course, of course; just what I was going to remark myself.'

'Have you guessed the riddle yet?' the Hatter said, turning to Alice again.

'No, I give it up,' Alice replied. 'What's the answer?'

'I haven't the slightest idea,' said the Hatter.

'Nor I,' said the March Hare.

Alice sighed wearily. 'I think you might do something better with the time,' she said, 'than waste it in asking riddles that have no answers.'

'If you knew Time as well as I do,' said the Hatter, 'you wouldn't talk about wasting *it*. It's *him*.'

'I don't know what you mean,' said Alice.

'Of course you don't!' the Hatter said, tossing his head contemptuously. 'I dare say you never even spoke to Time!'

'Perhaps not,' Alice cautiously replied: 'but I know I have to beat time when I learn music.'

'Ah! that accounts for it,' said the Hatter. 'He won't stand beating. Now, if you only kept on good terms with him, he'd do almost anything you liked with the clock. For instance, suppose it were nine o'clock in the morning, just time to begin lessons: you'd only have to whisper a hint to Time, and round goes the clock in a twinkling! Half-past one, time for dinner!'

('I only wish it was,' the March Hare said to itself in a whisper.)

'That would be grand, certainly,' said Alice thoughtfully: 'but then – I shouldn't be hungry for it, you know.'

'Not at first, perhaps,' said the Hatter: 'but you could keep it to half-past one as long as you liked.'

'Is that the way *you* manage?' Alice asked.

The Hatter shook his head mournfully. 'Not I!' he replied. 'We quarrelled last March – just before *he* went mad, you know –' (pointing with his tea-spoon at the March Hare) '– it was at the great concert given by the Queen of Hearts, and I had to sing:

"Twinkle, twinkle, little bat!
How I wonder what you're at!"

You know the song, perhaps?'

'I've heard something like it,' said Alice.

'It goes on, you know,' the Hatter continued, 'in this way:

"Up above the world you fly,
Like a tea-tray in the sky.
        Twinkle, twinkle –"'

Here the Dormouse shook itself, and began singing in its sleep '*Twinkle, twinkle, twinkle, twinkle –*' and went on so long that they had to pinch it to make it stop.

'Well, I'd hardly finished the first verse,' said the Hatter, 'when the Queen jumped up and bawled out, "He's murdering the time! Off with his head!"'

'How dreadfully savage!' exclaimed Alice.

'And ever since that,' the Hatter went on in a mournful tone, 'he won't do a thing I ask! It's always six o'clock now.'

A bright idea came into Alice's head. 'Is that the reason so many tea-things are put out here?' she asked.

'Yes, that's it,' said the Hatter with a sigh: 'it's always teatime, and we've no time to wash the things between whiles.'

'Then you keep moving round, I suppose?' said Alice.

'Exactly so,' said the Hatter: 'as the things get used up.'

'But what happens when you come to the beginning again?' Alice ventured to ask.

'Suppose we change the subject,' the March Hare interrupted, yawning. 'I'm getting tired of this. I vote the young lady tells us a story.'

HENRY LABOUCHÈRE
1831–1912

The Siege of Paris in 1870 by Prussian forces intent upon defeating Napoleon III's France was one of the defining events of the French capital. It lasted for five months, during which those residents who had not had the foresight to flee slowly starved. Henry Labouchère, a diplomat turned radical politician and journalist stayed in the city throughout, writing caustic articles for the *Daily News*, which he part-owned. They were later published as a book.

In this extract things are only just getting bad; by November richer residents were consuming the contents of the Paris zoos, while for the poor the price of rat was distressingly high. It shows Labouchère's awareness of inequality, even while he did not suffer. The siege ended in January, but was followed by the Paris Commune and La Semaine Sanglante (The Bloody Week), during which it is estimated that up to 10,000 people died, and part of the Louvre complex, the Tuileries Palace, was burnt down.

from *Diary of the Besieged Resident in Paris*

October 20th.

"The clients of M. Poiret are informed that they can only have one plate of meat," was the terrible writing which stared me on the wall, when I went to dine at my favourite bouillon—and, good heavens, what a portion it was! Not enough for the dinner of a fine lady who has previously gorged herself at a private luncheon. If meat is, as we are told, so plentiful that it will last for five weeks more, the mode in which it is distributed is radically bad. While at a large popular restaurant, where hundreds of the middle classes dine, each person only gets enough cat or horse to whet his appetite for more; in the expensive cafés on the Boulevards, feasts worthy of Lucullus are still served to those who are ready to part with their money with the proverbial readiness of fools. Far more practical, my worthy Republicans, would it be to establish "liberté, égalité, fraternité" in the cook shops, than to write the words in letters of gold over your churches. In every great city there always is much want and misery; here, although succour is supposed to be afforded to all who require it, many I fear are starving owing to that bureaucrat love of classification which is the curse of France. After my meagre dinner, I was strolling along the quays near

the river, *l'estomac* as *leger* as M. Ollivier's heart,
when I saw a woman leaning over the parapet. She
turned as I was passing her, and the lamp from the
opposite gate of the Tuileries shone on her face. It
was honest and homely, but so careworn, so utterly
hopeless, that I stopped to ask her if she was ill.
"Only tired and hungry," she replied; "I have been
walking all day, and I have not eaten since yesterday."
I took her to a café and gave her some bread and
coffee, and then she told me her story. She was a
peasant girl from Franche Comté, and had come to
Paris, where she had gone into service. But she had
soon tired of domestic servitude, and for the last year
she had supported herself by sewing waistcoats in a
great wholesale establishment. At the commence-
ment of the siege she had been discharged, and for
some days she found employment in a Government
workshop, but for the last three weeks she had wan-
dered here and there, vainly asking for work. One by
one she had sold every article of dress she possessed,
except the scanty garments she wore, and she had
lived upon bread and celery. The day before she had
spent her last sou, and when I saw her she had come
down to the river, starving and exhausted, to throw
herself into it. "But the water looked so cold, I did
not dare," she said. Thus spoke the grisette of Paris,
very different from the gay, thoughtless being of

French romance, who lives in a garret, her window shrouded with flowers, is adored by a student, and earns enough money in a few hours to pass the rest of the week dancing, gossiping, and amusing herself. As I listened to her, I felt ashamed of myself for repining because I had only had one plate of meat. The hopeless, desolate condition of this poor girl is that of many of her class to-day. But why should they complain? Is not King William the instrument of Heaven, and is he not engaged in a holy cause? That Kings should fight and that seamstresses should weep is in the natural order of things. Frenchmen and Frenchwomen only deserve to be massacred or starved if they are so lost to all sense of what is just as to venture to struggle against the dismemberment of their country, and do not understand how meet and right it is that their fellow-countrymen in Alsace should be converted into German subjects.

MARY ELIZABETH BRADDON
1835–1915

Another extract from Mary Elizabeth Braddon, this time from one of her more domestic novels (it still ends with the heroine in dark peril from a dastardly would-be rapist). Braddon's own life was in upheaval in 1875 due to her bigamous marriage to her publisher whose first wife was confined to an asylum. Once the scandal became public her staff all resigned and she and her husband had to move house to allow the gossip to wane.

The joy of this passage lies not only in the careful observation of the deleterious effect of a bad dinner on a good relationship, but in the detailed account of what it all cost. It is an ode to terrible food, and the reader cannot help but feel Herman's sadness at the wasted opportunity.

from *Hostages to Fortune*

They are to dine at half-past seven. At six the parlour-maid brings her a wishy-washy cup of tea, and a thin slice of new bread thickly buttered. This refreshment fails to revive her spirits, and she finds herself lapsing into melaneholy on this first day of her home life.

But at last, just as she comes down-stairs in her simple dinner dress, a latchkey sounds in the hall-door, and Herman appears. Happy meeting, fond welcome, as after a severance of years.

"Why, my love, you look pale and tired," he says, as they go into the library together. "You haven't been over-exerting yourself about domestic duties, I hope?"

"O no, dear; only—"

"Only what, my pet?"

"The day has seemed so long and dull without you."

"Has it, darling?" he exclaims, pleased by the avowal. "I oughtn't to have gone to town the first day, perhaps; only I was anxious to see Standish about my novel, and to hear what had been doing in the last six weeks. You went for a walk, I hope?"

"What, alone, Herman, in this strange place!"

"Ah, to be sure—you don't know the neighbourhood yet. There are some nice walks—Barnes Common, for instance, not above half an hour's walk from here; and Wimbledon, almost as near; I must show you them next week. And now I'll go and wash my hands for dinner. I've eaten no lunch, on purpose to do justice to our first home dinner."

"I hope it will be nice, dear; but the cook is rather young. However, she seems to understand things, and is very confident."

The table in the Pompeian chamber looks pretty enough, with the fragile modern glass and heavy old silver—the last the Squire's gift to his daughter— when Herman and his wife go into dinner presently; but the dinner itself is a failure, and Herman resents the fact more intensely than Editha would have expected from a poet.

The soles are burned on the outside and pink within; the fowls are the oldest and toughest birds Herman has encountered for some time, and Swiss poultry has not been always young; the ham is half raw, hard, and salt; the pheasants are reduced to a condition in which the flesh crumbles off their bones; the bread-sauce is watery; the gravy is chiefly remarkable for grease, Lee and Perrin, and black pepper; the pastry is a leaden sarcophagus, in which a few half-cooked apples are entombed; the custards are curdled. But happily, before they arrive at this stage of the feast, Herman has spoiled an excellent appetite with a series of disappointments, and has retired within himself.

O, those nice little club dinners—so simple, so inexpensive! The one whiting, crisp and of a golden brown, with his tail in his mouth—delicate symbol of eternity; the longitudinal slice of haunch, roasted by a cook who has elevated roasting to a science. Herman is not so practical as to count the cost of this first home dinner, or he would find the account sadly against domesticity.

Soles	.	.	.	.	.	.	£0	2	6
Fowls	.	.	.	.	.	.	0	7	6
Ham	.	.	.	.	.	.	0	13	7½
Pheasants	.	.	.	.	.	.	0	8	0
Gravy-beef, vegetables, eggs, butter, lard, and sundries .	.	0	5	0
Total	.	.	.	.	.	.	£1	16	7½

His dinner at the club would have cost him three-and-sixpence; but then he cannot take Editha to a club, and it is an established principle in the British mind that to dine out of doors is adverse to the best interests of domestic life.

"I am afraid you have not enjoyed your dinner, dear," Editha says nervously, when the parlour-maid, who is slow and stately in her movements, has swept the last crumb from the tablecloth, and withdrawn her attentive ear from Mr. and Mrs. Westray's conversation.

"We won't call it dinner, Editha. Everything was simply uneatable. You must tell your cook so tomorrow; and if she can't do better, you must dismiss her. There must be plenty of good cooks to be had, if you go the right way to work."

Editha sighs. It seems a bad beginning somehow, insignificant as the matter is to her mind. Herman drinks a couple of glasses of claret, conquers a disposition towards ill-temper, and they retire to the pretty little study, where there is a cheery fire on this dull October evening, and sit opposite each other on either side of the hearth like old-established married people, and Editha is happy again.

ABBY FISHER
1831–1890

British rule in America ended in the 1780s, but the inhumane system of slavery they had introduced remained in place until 1865. African Americans continued to be regarded as legally inferior for over a century, and the legacy of slavery sadly still leaves its mark today. For many years thought to be the earliest cookery book by an African American, several books pre-date Abby Fisher's. However, it remains important, both for its publishing history and its excellent recipes. The book was dictated by Fisher (who was illiterate), to a committee, which in part explains the idiosyncratic spelling. It was published by a woman's co-operative. Fisher herself was a successful cook and caterer, winning awards for her preserves. Her book includes a number of recipes for dishes now regarded as part of the lexicon of the cookery of the Deep South. She was almost certainly born a slave.

from *What Mrs. Fisher Knows About Old Southern Cooking*

The publication of a book on my knowledge and experience of Southern Cooking, Pickle and Jelly Making, has been frequently asked of me by my lady friends and patrons in San Francisco and Oakland, and also by ladies of Sacramento during the State Fair in 1879. Not being able to read or write myself, and my husband also having been without the advantages of an education—upon whom would devolve the writing of the book at my dictation—caused me to doubt whether I would be able to present a work that would give perfect satisfaction. But, after due consideration, I concluded to bring forward a book of my knowledge—based on an experience of upwards of thirty-five years—in the art of cooking Soups, Gumbos, Terrapin Stews, Meat Stews, Baked and Roast Meats, Pastries, Pies and Biscuits, making Jellies, Pickles, Sauces, Ice-Creams and Jams, preserving Fruits, etc. The book will be found a complete instructor, so that a child can understand it and learn the art of cooking.

Respectfully,

MRS. ABBY FISHER,

Late of Mobile, Ala.

FRIED CHICKEN.

Cut the chicken up, separating every joint, and wash clean. Salt and pepper it, and roll into flour well. Have your fat very hot, and drop the pieces into it, and let them cook brown. The chicken is done when the fork passes easily into it. After the chicken is all cooked, leave a little of the hot fat in the skillet; then take a tablespoonful of dry flour and brown it in the fat, stirring it around, then pour water in and stir till the gravy is as thin as soup.

OCHRA GUMBO.

Get a beef shank, have it cracked and put to boil in one gallon of water. Boil to half a gallon, then strain and put back on fire. Cut ochra in small pieces and put in soup; don't put in any ends of ochra. Season with salt and pepper while cooking. Stir it occasionally and keep it from burning. To be sent to table with dry boiled rice. Never stir rice while boiling. Season rice always with salt when it is first put on to cook, and do not have too much water in rice while boiling.

SWEET POTATO PIE.

Two pounds of potatoes will make two pies. Boil the potatoes soft; peel and mash fine through a cullender while hot; one tablespoonful of butter to be

mashed in with the potato. Take five eggs and beat
the yelks and whites separate and add one gill of
milk; sweeten to taste; squeeze the juice of one
orange, and grate one-half of the peel into the liquid.
One half teaspoonful of salt in the potatoes. Have
only one crust and that at the bottom of the plate.
Bake quickly.

CREOLE CHOW CHOW.

One gallon of green tomatoes, sliced thin, half dozen
silver skin onions, sliced thin, one gallon wine vinegar, two tea-cups of brown sugar, one tablespoonful
of cayenne pepper, one tablespoonful black pepper,
one tablespoonful of tumerick. Put the onions and
tomatoes together in a keg or jar and sprinkle over
them one pint of salt and let it so remain twenty-
four hours, then drain all the brine off from them
over cullender, then put the vinegar to them and add
the seasoning, and put to cook on a slow fire, stir to
keep from burning. It will take the whole day to
cook; you can make any quantity you want, by doub-
ling the quantity of vegetables and seasonings here
prescribed, or if you want a less quantity, lessen the
proportion, say half the quantity, then you want a
half gallon of tomatoes to begin with, and a half of
every thing else needed in this chow chow.

Take the melon rind and scrape all the meat from the inside, and then carefully slice all the outside of rind from the white part of the rind, then lay or cover the white part over with salt. It will have to remain under salt one week before pickling; the rind will keep in salt from year to year. When you want to pickle it, take it from the salt and put into clear water, change the water three times a day—must be changed say every four hours—then take the rind from water and dry it with a clean cloth. Have your vinegar boiling, and put the rind into it and let it scald four minutes, then take it off the fire and let it lay in vinegar four days; then take it from the vinegar, drain, and sprinkle sugar thickly over it and let it remain so one day. To make syrup, take the syrup from the rind and add eight pounds more sugar to it, and put to boil; boil till a thick and clear syrup. Weigh ten pounds of rind to twelve pounds of sugar; cover the rind with four pounds of it and make the syrup with the remaining eight pounds. While the syrup is cooking add one teacupful of white ginger root and the peel of three lemons. When the syrup is cooked, then put the rind into the boiling syrup, and let it cook till you can pass a fork through it with ease, then it is done. When cooled put in jar or bottles with one pint of vinegar to one quart of syrup, thus the pickle is made. See that they be well covered with vinegar and syrup as directed.

TERRAPIN STEW.

Always have the female terrapins, and put them alive in boiling water. Let them remain for fifteen minutes and then take the shells from them, being careful not to break the galls. Clean the entrails from the meat, and scrape the black skin from the feet with a knife. Half a dozen terrapins will serve twelve persons. After thoroughly cleaning the terrapins, lay them in clear water for ten minutes, and then put them in a kettle to stew with half a pint of water, and stew very slowly for about three hours. Boil half a dozen eggs hard, and rub the yelks to a powder. Then add half a pound of best butter to the eggs and beat together until it becomes a cream. To this cream add one pint of sherry wine and mix it well. Then add this preparation to the stew very gradually, stirring well, so as to thoroughly mix it in. While the stew is cooking, mix a teaspoonful of best mustard to a tablespoonful of wine and put in. Slice one lemon and add to stew just before dishing it up for table. Three hours is sufficient time to cook it. You had better put the wine in the stew and not mix it with the eggs, for fear you may not mix it in right and that there may be no mistake. With the above directions you have a perfect stew, A teacupful of sweet cream is an improvement, if you like it: also a dozen grains of allspice. Salt and pepper to taste.

❦

AGNES MARSHALL
1855–1905

Cookery book writer, inventor and entrepreneur, Agnes Marshall was an indefatigable and very important figure on the late-Victorian culinary scene. She ran a cookery school, edited the *Table* magazine, and lectured widely as well as publishing four books. This, *The Book of Ices*, was her first, and it is with the history of ice cream that she is most associated.

Victorian ices came in an astonishing variety of flavours, and Marshall's recipes are innovative and exciting. Ices were habitually served as part of the dessert course, intended as a palate cleanser, to rejuvenate jaded diners. This one is reminiscent of eighteenth-century (and earlier) tarts and puddings, which used spinach less for flavour than for its vivid green colour in an era before chemical food dyes. Marshall, who also sold such modernities as artificial colours and flavourings, adds a little extra colour just in case.

'Iced Spinach à la Crème',
from *The Book of Ices*

ICED SPINACH À LA CRÈME
(*EPINARDS GLACÉES À LA CRÈME*)

Put 2 or 3 handfuls of spinach in cold water with salt, and a very tiny pinch of soda; let it come to the boil; strain off and press the water from it. Boil half a pint of milk and stir it on to 4 yolks of eggs, and put it on the stove again to thicken—don't let it boil; add a little apple green to colour it, and to half a pint of the custard add a small dessert-spoonful of castor sugar and a pinch of salt; mix with the spinach, pass through the tammy, and freeze; add, when partly frozen, half a teacupful of whipped cream sweetened with a very slight dust of castor sugar. Freeze dry and mould in a Neapolitan box in the cave for about 1½ hours; then cut out in cutlet shapes. Dish on a border of iced cream, and iced cream for the centre; for this use 1 pint of cream, 1 dessert-spoonful of castor sugar, ditto of orange flower water, and a few drops of vanilla. Freeze dry and mould in a border mould.

Fanny Lemira Gillette & Hugo Ziemann

1828–1926 & 1853–1904

The White House Cookbook (1887) was one of the must-have books of its day for aspiring society hostesses – including the inhabitants of the White House itself. The first edition was by Fanny Lemira Gillette, who described herself as having made a 'lifelong and thorough study of cookery and housekeeping', specifically for American homes. It had only a very tangential connection to the White House. For the second edition she combined forces with Hugo Ziemann, a White House steward and renowned French chef. His insights into the inner workings of the presidential palace were one of the selling points of the book.

This extract is from the section on polite behaviour. The late nineteenth century saw an explosion of advice books, particularly those which guided the uninitiated through the pitfalls of society at a slightly higher level than s/he was used to. However, the very possession of an etiquette book was a giveaway. For many, if you weren't born to it, you had no right to be doing it.

'Table Etiquette',
from *The White House Cookbook*

SMALL POINTS ON TABLE ETIQUETTE.

Delicacy of manner at table stamps both man and woman, for one can, at a glance, discern whether a person has been trained to eat well—*i. e.* to hold the knife and fork properly, to eat without the slightest sound of the lips, to drink quietly, to use the napkin rightly, to make no noise with any of the implements of the table, and last, but not least, to eat slowly and masticate the food thoroughly. All these points should be most carefully taught to children, and then they will always feel at their ease at the grandest tables in the land. There is no position where the innate refinement of a person is more fully exhibited than at the table, and nowhere that those who have not been trained in table etiquette feel more keenly their deficiencies. The knife should never be used to carry food to the mouth, but only to cut it up into small mouthfuls; then place it upon the plate at one side, and take the fork in the right hand, and eat all the food with it. When both have been used finally, they should be laid diagonally across the plate, with both handles towards the right hand; this is understood by well-trained waiters, to be the signal for removing them, together with the plate.

Be careful to keep the mouth shut closely while masticating the food. It is the opening of the lips which causes the smacking which seems very disgusting. Chew your food well, but do it silently, and be careful to take small mouthfuls. The knife can be used to cut the meat finely, as large pieces of meat are not healthful, and appears very indelicate. At many tables, two, three or more knives and forks are placed on the table, the knives at the right hand of the plate, the forks at the left,—a knife and a fork for each course, so that there need be no replacing of them after the breakfast or dinner is served. The smaller ones, which are for game, dessert, or for hot cakes at breakfast, can be tucked under the edges of the plate, and the large ones, for the meat and vegetables, are placed outside of them. Be very careful not to clatter your knives and forks upon your plates, but use them without noise. When you are helped to anything, *do not* wait until the rest of the company are provided, it is not considered good breeding. When passing the plate for a second helping, lay them together at one side of the plate, with handles to the right. Soup is always served for the first course, and it should be eaten with dessert spoons, and taken from the sides, not the tips of them, without any sound of the lips, and not sucked into the mouth audibly from the ends of the spoon. Bread should not be broken into soup or gravy. Never ask to be helped to soup a second time. The hostess may ask you to take a second plate, but you will politely decline. Fish chowder, which is served in soup plates, is said to be an exception which proves this rule, and when eating of that it is correct to take a second plateful, if desired.

Another generally neglected obligation is that of spreading butter on one's bread as it lies in one's plate, or but slightly lifted at one end of the plate; it is very frequently buttered in the air, bitten in gouges, and still held in the face and eyes of the table with the marks of the teeth on it. This is certainly not altogether pleasant, and it is better to cut it, a bit at a time, after buttering it, and put piece by piece in the mouth with one's finger and thumb. Never help yourself to butter, or any other food with your own knife or fork. It is not considered good taste to mix food on the same plate. Salt must be left on the side of the plate and never on the table-cloth.

❦

MARY KROUT
1851–1927

Mary Hannah Krout was a leading American journalist and fierce advocate of women's suffrage. She
combined her travels with lecturing on women's
rights as well as writing articles. She was the staff
correspondent for the *Chicago Inter-Ocean* from 1895
to 1898, and she published her articles, which included observations on the Diamond Jubilee, as a
book in 1899.

In this extract, she casts an outsider's view on the
way food is procured and prepared in London, and
on the contrast between British and American food.
Much of what she describes is not unfamiliar today.
The boy hauling ice would probably have been
delivering it to a household desirous of making ice
cream (ice mixed with salt was used as a freezing
agent). The ice was imported from North America
or Canada.

from *A Looker-On in London*

By the first of July the heated term makes itself felt – not the glaring, torrid heat with winds like the simoon – but humid, stifling weather, during which the sky is occasionally veiled in pale grey clouds. For some occult reason the temperature at 85 degrees is much more oppressive, even to Americans who are inured to the tropics, than a greater degree of heat in the United States. And if the sojourning American feels discomfort, the native Londoner perspires, and gasps, and even dies from sunstroke, or what he calls "heat apoplexy." He resorts to every means of relief of which he can avail himself, except the use of ice. One may perceive, however, that prejudice even in this last extreme is giving way. American "ice-cream soda" is now offered in various fashionable restaurants in Regent Street and elsewhere, and, with the throngs of American tourists that frequent them, partaking of the familiar refreshment of their native land, increasing numbers of English may be seen also consuming the cooling beverage with somewhat disapproving satisfaction. Most significant of all – I saw a lad, one blazing August morning, hauling a block of ice in a hand-cart down Sloane street. It was remarkable to see the ice in the first place, and there was an added touch of the unique in the fact that upon the crystal tube had been fastened, in some manner, a neat placard bearing the name and address of the purchaser. This was a precaution which had been taken to secure its safe delivery to the proper owner, as the average Englishman would not receive under his roof that which we consider one of the necessaries of life and to which he attributes the whole of our national dyspepsia.

While recent shipments of California fruit have sold readily enough in the London market, it is doubtful if it will ever attain very high favor; it is thought that its flavor has been sacrificed to size, and that it is hardly equal to the native fruit which appeals less pleasingly to the eye. The English fruit crop is comparatively small, but that which is produced cannot be surpassed for delicate and exquisite flavor. English and Scotch strawberries are beyond compare, so large that one berry will furnish several mouthfuls, sweet as honey and almost seedless. The goose-berry, which we scarcely respect, is luscious and delicious, as big as plums and almost as sweet as the strawberry.

The English are much too sensible to cook fruit, except that which is buried in the yawning caverns of the tart; the most of it comes to the table in the natural state, in plates prettily decorated with a border of leaves. Fruit constitutes what is technically called

the dessert – a term which we use indiscriminately –
as distinguished from the sweets that precede it – the
starchy blanc mange, jelly stiffened with Irish moss,
the solid and uncompromising pudding, and the tart
aforesaid. English apples, except a few choice and
costly varieties are altogether contemptible in appearance, but are very deceiving. They are like plain
girls of whom it is said, "they are not pretty, but they
are good." The smallest, knottiest and most unprom-
ising may be found to possess qualities that many of
our larger and more richly colored varieties wholly
lack, and they are as fragrant as sweet-briar.

In 1895 an unprecedented crop was produced;
the boughs bent and broke under the weight of fruit
and the ground was thickly strewn with it, but prices
were so low that the farmer could make nothing by
sending it to market. Hundreds of bushels went to
waste, for cider making is now almost an unknown
industry, so rare are the seasons in which it is prac-
ticable.

English plums cannot be surpassed; I saw a tree
weighted down with what, from a fleeting glimpse
through a railway carriage window, appeared to be
crimson pears. They were plums with a pinkish
crimson skin, a rich yellow pulp within, sweet and
finely flavored. English pears, especially those grown
upon espaliers, are fully equal to our own best var-

ieties. Peaches and grapes which ripen only under glass are beautiful in form and color, but they are disappointing, the peaches especially being somewhat insipid. English vegetables are exceptionally good, lettuce and celery being crisp and with a nutty sweetness. As to the food in general, it is all good, but there is a sameness, even in its very excellence, of which one tires. There are few valid grounds for complaint; one would like once in a while to find fault with heavy rolls or sour bread; tough steak, tough chops and stringy beef are also apparently unknown; one may find some relief in criticising the potatoes which are seldom thoroughly cooked and denouncing the practice of stewing mint with peas – a combination that is thoroughly distasteful to the untrained palate. The soup is above reproach; so is the fish with its inevitable egg sauce; the fowl with its attendant bread sauce, its gizzard neatly tucked under one wing and the liver under the other, throwing a flood of light on that unintelligible phrase, "the liver wing," which occurs in English novels. The English tart has been mentioned, but apparently it will not down; it might be described as of the Tudor style of architecture, and is so big and strong and solid that it impresses the unfamiliar mind as having been built by government contract.

It is a matter of some wonder to the American

why the English should enjoy an apparent monopoly of two things that ought to be within reach of all people of limited means – sharp knives and thin bread and butter. Both are practically unknown on our side of the Atlantic, and I remember reading in Crabbe Robinson's Diary how he vainly endeavored to instruct his Spanish friend, Madame Mosquera, in the art of cutting bread and butter, when she was called upon to entertain Lord and Lady Holland who arrived unexpectedly in Corrunna with the English fleet.

"That there might be no mistake," he writes, "I requested a loaf to be brought and I actually cut a couple of slices as thin as wafers, directing that a plate should be filled with such." Notwithstanding his efforts, he goes on to relate that "after the guests arrived a huge salver was set forth resembling in size the charger on which the head of John the Baptist is usually brought by Herod's step daughter. On this was a huge silver dish piled up with great pieces of bread and butter an inch thick, sufficient to feed Westminster school."

English bread and butter, like English lawns, must be regarded as hereditary and indigenous – the outgrowth of national character and of centuries of custom. English tea, to those who like tea, is delicious, but a cup of good coffee is a thing almost unknown. Except the tiny cup of black coffee which is brought into the drawing-room after dinner, people rarely drink it. That which comes upon the breakfast table is usually of a pale purplish hue, of attenuated weakness and with a faint flavor of licorice; for general unpalatableness it can be matched only in our Western farm houses, where the art of cooking is still rudimentary. A vivacious American who lived in certain Kensington Mansions remarked, with an extravagance of speech that one need not accept literally:

"I am so tired of joints, and boiled vegetables, and milky puddings that I would give my immortal soul for a good American dinner."

She expressed herself strongly, but she had lived in London five years and was homesick. The aversion to our cookery is just as marked on the part of visiting English, and there are very few who do not long for the roast beef of their own land: Sala – an epicure of pronounced fastidiousness – liked nothing but our oysters; and a young English girl who sojourned for a time in Kansas made this confession: "The food was absolutely uneatable, don't you know; and it was served in a lot of little dishes like birds' bath-tubs."

The fish in the London markets are unsurpassed, salmon, sole and plaice being the preferred varieties;

the oysters, even the much-vaunted native, are small and coppery.

The ham and bacon deserve their reputation, and fresh eggs are good when they are what they profess to be. There was once a belief that the date stamped in blue letters on an egg related to the date upon which it was removed from the nest, but there have been occasions when there was self-evident reason to believe that the date had nothing to do with the actual age of the egg. It should be said that the practice of breaking an egg into a cup and mixing it up, white and yolk, with salt and pepper, at table, is looked upon as a barbarous and sickening proceeding, and Americans aspiring to shine in English society should take a careful course of instruction in eating their eggs according to established usage, before buying their steamer ticket.

ELIZABETH ROBBINS PENNELL
1855–1936

The Feasts of Autolcyus: The Diary of a Greedy Woman
is a collection of essays on food written originally for
the *Pall Mall Gazette*. Their author, Elizabeth Robbins
Pennell, was an American journalist who had settled
in London. She wrote on a variety of topics, but is
best known for her art criticism, travelogues (she
was a keen cyclist) and her food writing.

Pennell and her husband ran a literary salon from
their London home, and were well connected in the
fashionable artistic set. She was a significant collector of recipe books, both contemporary and
historic. This extract is typical of the whimsical, lyr-
ical style in which she wrote, underlain with a solid
appreciation of a well-thought-out recipe, and a
delicious plate of food. The book was reissued with
a less honest title in 1901, as *The Delights of Delicate
Eating*.

'The Simple Sole',
from *Feasts of Autolycus*

Have you ever considered the sole: the simple, unassuming sole, in Quaker-like garb, striking a quiet grey note in every fishmonger's window, a constant rebuke to the mackerel that makes such vain parade of its green audacity, of the lobster that flaunts its scarlet boldness in the face of the passer-by? By its own merits the sole appeals; upon no meretricious charm does it base its claim for notice. Flat and elusive, it seems to seek retirement, to beg to be forgotten. And yet, year by year, it goes on, unostentatiously and surely increasing in price; year by year, it establishes, with firm hold, its pre-eminence upon the *menu* of every well-regulated *table d'hôte*.

But here pause a moment, and reflect. For it is this very *table d'hôte* which bids fair to be the sole's undoing. If it has been maligned and misunderstood, it is because, swaddled in bread-crumbs, fried in indifferent butter, it has come to be the symbol of hotel or pension dinner, until the frivolous and heedless begin to believe that it cannot exist otherwise, that in its irrepressible bread-crumbs it must swim through the silent sea.

The conscientious *gourmand* knows better, however. He knows that bread-crumbs and frying-pan are but mere child's play compared to its diviner devices. It has been said that the number and various shapes of fishes are not "more strange or more fit for contemplation than their different natures, inclinations, and actions." But fitter subject still for the contemplative, and still more strange, is their marvellous, well-nigh limitless, culinary ambition. Triumph after triumph the most modest of them all yearns to achieve, and if this sublime yearning be ever and always suppressed and thwarted and misdoubted, the fault lies with dull, plodding, unenterprising humans. Not one yearns to such infinite purpose as the sole; not one is so snubbed and enslaved. A very Nora among fish, how often must it long to escape and to live its own life—or, to be more accurate, to die its own death!

Not that bread-crumbs and frying-pan are not all very well in their way. Given a discreet cook, pure virginal butter, a swift fire, and a slice of fresh juicy lemon, something not far short of perfection may be reached. But other ways there are, more suggestive, more inspiring, more godlike. Turn to the French *chef* and learn wisdom from him.

First and foremost in this glorious repertory comes *sole à la Normande*, which, under another name, is the special distinction and pride of the

Restaurant Marguery. Take your sole—from the waters of Dieppe would you have the best—and place it, with endearing, lover-like caress, in a pretty earthenware dish, with butter for only companion. At the same time, in sympathetic saucepan, lay mussels to the number of two dozen, opened and well cleaned, as a matter of course; and let each rejoice in the society of a stimulating mushroom; when almost done, but not quite, make of them a garland round the expectant sole: cover their too seductive beauty with a rich white sauce; rekindle their passion in the oven for a few minutes; and serve immediately and hot. Joy is the result; pure, uncontaminated joy. If this be too simple for your taste, then court elaboration and more complex sensation after this fashion: from the first, unite the sole to two of its most devoted admirers, the oyster and the mussel—twelve, say, of each—and let thyme and fragrant herbs and onion and white wine and truffles be close witnesses of their union. Seize the sole when it is yet but half cooked; stretch it out gently in another dish, to which oysters and mussels must follow in hot, precipitate flight. And now the velling sauce, again white, must have calf's kidney and salt pork for foundation, and the first gravy of the fish for fragrance and seasoning. Mushrooms and lemon in slices may be added to the garniture. And if at the first mouthful you do not thrill with rapture, the Thames will prove scarce deep and muddy enough to hide your shame.

Put to severest test, the love of the sole for the oyster is never betrayed. Would you be convinced— and it is worth the trouble—experiment with *sole farcie aux hutlers*, a dish so perfect that surely, like manna, it must have come straight from Heaven. In prosaic practical language, it is thus composed: you stuff your sole with forcemeat of oysters and truffles, you season with salt and carrot and lemon, you steep it in white wine—not sweet, or the sole is dishonoured—you cook it in the oven, and you serve the happy fish on a rich *ragoût* of the oysters and truffles. Or, another tender conceit that you may make yours to your own great profit and enlightenment, is *sole farcie aux crevettes*. In this case it is wise to fillet the sole and wrap each fillet about the shrimps, which have been well mixed and pounded with butter. A rich *Béchamel* sauce and garniture of lemons complete a composition so masterly that, before it, as before a fine Velasquez, criticism is silenced.

ℰ

ANON.
'She Cooked the Dinner', 1900

This anonymous poem was published in *Food &
Cookery*, the magazine of the Universal Cookery &
Food Association. The UC&FA was a members'
organization, set up by a group of chefs led by
Charles Herman Senn, a Swiss author and chef. Its
members included top hotel chefs and royal chefs,
and also many hundreds of men and women toiling
away in the lower reaches of the profession.

Each issue of *Food & Cookery* contained a variety
of articles, from discussions of the best way to cater
for vegetarians, to a robust defence of British cooks.
It habitually included example menus from grand
occasions, new recipes, and reports on culinary
shows. It also had more left-field items, of which this
is an excellent example.

The content, really, needs no further explanation.

'She Cooked the Dinner'

He sat at the dinner table
    With a discontented frown;
The potatoes and steak were underdone,
    And the bread was baked too brown;
The pie was too sour, the pudding too sweet,
    And the beef was much too fat;
The soup so greasy, too, and salt,
    'Twas was hardley fit for the cat.

"I wish you could eat the bread and pie
    I've seen my mother make;
They are something like, and 'twould do you good
    Just to look at a slice of her cake."
Said the smiling wife, "I'll improve with age,
    Just now I'm but a beginner;
But your mother has come to visit us,
    And to-day she cooked the dinner."

                      —*Tit Bits.*

GABRIEL TSCHUMI
1883–1957

One of the only sources of information on life in the royal kitchens at the end of Victoria's reign, Gabriel Tschumi's autobiography is a fascinating glimpse into life in royal service. Tschumi entered the kitchens as an apprentice, aged sixteen, in 1898. His memories are really those of the next reign, that of Edward VII, during which he rose up the ranks. He later moved to cook for the Duke of Portland before returning to royal service under the now-widowed Queen Mary.

This extract recounts the below-stairs reaction to the sudden illness of Edward VII on the eve of his coronation in 1902. Prince Albert had reorganized the way in which leftovers were distributed from the palaces, with an eye to fairness and no waste, and this is indicative of how seamlessly the system worked.

from *Royal Chef*

Finally a suitable menu was prepared. The fourteen courses were submitted to King Edward and Queen Alexandra, written out carefully by M. Menager, for approval long before June. They had been passed, and the King sent down a message that he was very pleased with the menu for the banquet. The coronation orders were placed with tradespeople—2,500 plump quails, 300 legs of mutton, 80 chickens, and a host of other orders. There was to be sturgeon, foie gras, caviare and asparagus. On the fish course was sole garnished with five different types of garnishing. For dessert there were liqueur jellies and *Caisses de fraises Miramare*, a strawberry dish which took three days to prepare, both for the confectioners who made the baskets of sugar holding the dessert and the cooks who made the jellied strawberries and vanilla cream mixture of which it consisted. It was not always a happy arrangement to bring in extra chefs to assist with preparations, but in view of the work required a small number had been engaged for the week preceding the coronation. We had to go ahead with the coronation banquet menu in between preparing the daily meals at the Palace, and the only time when we could be really free to work on it was in the evenings, so most of us agreed to work late for a week or two.

It had not been a good week. Everyone knew King Edward was not well, and special light dishes had been prepared for him separately at lunch and dinner, which meant extra work. It was quite hot for June, and the younger ones amongst us felt restless and impatient to escape from the heat of the kitchens into the cooler evening air. M. Menager sensed this, and because he appreciated how irksome all the early preparations for such a large banquet can be he disliked insisting that everyone worked harder than usual and became irritable simply because it was necessary to insist. There are bound to be small hitches in arranging a big royal banquet, and one of the most annoying of these had delayed some of the cooks. The order for caviare from Russia for the banquet had arrived, and in some inexplicable way the checking of it was overlooked. When it came to be needed we found that through an error of calculation there was only half the quantity necessary. M. Menager was very angry, and the Clerk of the Kitchens denied that the error was his. Eventually the matter was sorted out and the extra amount obtained, but this small hitch did not make things any easier amongst the staff.

At last almost everything was ready. The jellies

had been made to take the cold quail and other dishes, some flavoured with claret and brandy, and some to be used as dessert with liqueur. They filled almost every available dish in the kitchens which could be set aside for coronation banquet use, and we were looking forward to the time when the kitchen routine settled down to normal again. I had been working on the *Consommé de faisan aux quencllies* with which the banquet was to begin. It had been clarified and awaited only the red, white and green quenelles or forcemeat garnishing which were to give it the appropriate banquet touch. Almost half the kitchens had been taken over for coronation dishes.

Once again on the night before the coronation we were to work late on the sauces and croquettes needed for the following day. We were about to begin, when word came to us that the King's doctor Sir Frederick Treves had been summoned hurriedly to Buckingham Palace, and after spending several hours with the King had had a consultation with the Master of the Household, Lord Farquhar. He in turn had hurried to see the Clerk Controller, and there were rumours that the King was very ill and might not be able to attend Westminster Abbey for his crowning after all. M. Menager grew pale, for he was an old Palace servant and deeply devoted to the King, but as we had heard nothing official we decided to carry on with our work. About a quarter of an hour later the Clerk Controller sent for the Royal Chef. When he returned we learned that King Edward had been taken very ill that day and was to undergo an operation as soon as possible. As a result the coronation and banquet were to be postponed until his health had recovered.

The staff listened to the news in silence. It took a little time to get used to the fact that the King, who was no longer a young man, was in such serious health. But once we had adapted ourselves to the change in plans a problem faced us. What was to be done with the food for the banquet of two hundred and fifty guests?

Some of it could be kept in the ice-boxes, but a lot of it was perishable and would not keep. There was also the difficulty of storing all the jellies, which could not remain in the dishes which were filled to overflowing. These days at Buckingham Palace such a problem would not arise, for they could be stored in screw-top jars indefinitely. But such modern preserving utensils did not exist in King Edward VII's reign, and we had never faced such a large-scale storing operation before. Finally the Clerk of the Kitchens redeemed himself in everyone's eyes by coming up with a solution. The jellies could be melted down and stored in magnum champagne bottles until such time as the coronation banquet took place. When they were needed they could be remelted by being put in front of the fire and then returned to moulds. We spent the next few hours carrying out this course of action, and eventually there were two hundred and fifty champagne bottles of claret and liqueur jelly ranged along the wall in one corner of the kitchens.

This was by no means an end to the problem. The caviare could be kept on ice, and it was possible to preserve the two thousand five hundred quails. But there were huge amounts of cooked chicken, partridge, sturgeon and cutlets, not to mention all the fruit and cream dessert which would not keep. A little could be put aside for the staff, but the rest, it was decided, would have to be given to charitable organisations dealing with the poor.

We were in touch with a good many of these charities, who had literally thousands of hungry and homeless families on their books, and the Buckingham Palace staff often passed on to them broken or spoilt food. In this case they would be receiving something a little different—six or seven courses from the coronation banquet of a King—and from all the many charities it was hard to choose one which could be relied on to handle the disposition of the food fairly and discreetly. Finally we stored the food in hampers for the Sisters of the Poor, and, without any explanation of how it came to be passed on, gave it to them to distribute to poor families around Whitechapel and the East End. It was sad to think we would never know how the dishes we had laboured over for more than a fortnight had been received, and in the Household disorganisation caused by the King's illness few people gave a thought to the coronation banquet and what had happened to the food prepared for it. But on June 26, the date the banquet was to have been held, it was the poor of Whitechapel and not foreign kings, princes and diplomats who had the *Consommé de faisan aux quenelles, Cotelettes de bécassines à la Souvaroff* and many of the other dishes created by the Royal Chef and his staff to grace the King's coronation.

❦

GEORGE SIMS
1847–1922

George Sims is best known as a journalist and satirist who wrote both for the stage and print media. Although comfortably middle class, he had a strong social conscience which led him to become a campaigner for social reform. Much of his literary output centred on this theme and he helped raise public awareness of the plight of the urban poor. In 1880, he co-founded a charity devoted to providing free meals for children.

Living London was one of several books Sims wrote which explored the streets of London. In this extract Sims considers street vendors who were ubiquitous across London, for even the middle classes were fond of hot rolls or ice cream. However, the majority operated in the East End, and were often the only source of hot food residents had access to. Eels were particularly popular, and, off the street, eel-pie and mash shops were very common, although few remain today.

'London's Light Refreshments', from *Living London*

It is in the evening that the fried fish and potato "chip" shop, the ham and beef shop, and the cook-shop, whose specialities are the hot sausage and the cooked onion and mashed potato, do a busy trade. Before the windows of these establishments there is generally a small crowd, not necessarily hungry, but interested. You may see among them well dressed and well-to-do people. For to watch the savoury sausage sizzle, and the odoriferous onion ooze its oiliness in the pan laid over a gas arrangement, is a delight to most of us. Pork chops and tomatoes have frequently cooking pans of their own in these shop windows, but I hesitate to include a pork chop in a catalogue of light refreshments.

The eel-pie shop is not as fascinating, but is almost as well patronised. The dressing of an eel-pie shop window is conservative. It is a tradition handed down through many generations to the present day. The eels are shown artistically in lengths on a bed of parsley which is spread over a dish. On either side of the eels cold pies in their pans are laid in tempting profusion but in perfect order. The eel-pie shop varies its menu. You may procure at the same establishment cranberry tarts, and at some of them apple tarts; also meat pies and meat puddings, and at the Christmas season mince pies.

To see the eel-pie business at its best, to appreciate its poetry, you must watch the process of serving its customers. Behind the counter on a busy night stands the proprietor in his shirt sleeves, a clean white apron preserving his waistcoat and nether garments from damage. Observe with what nimble deftness he lifts the lid of the metal receptacle in front of him, whips out a hot pie, runs a knife round it inside the dish, and turns it out on to a piece of paper for the customer—possibly into the eager outstretched hand.

He is generally assisted by his wife and daughter, who are almost, but not equally, dexterous. There are metal receptacles in front of them also, and the pies are whipped out in such rapid succession that your eyes become dazzled by the quick continuous movement. If you watch long enough it will almost appear to you that a shower of hot pies is being flung up from below by an invisible agency.

The oyster shop is not as common as it was in the days when natives were sixpence a dozen. But there are many scattered about London still. The great oyster rooms are at the west. At one you can have fish in every variety, and lobster salad and dressed crabs are a specialty. There is one famous establishment near Regent Street whose oysters and fish sandwiches attract the highest in the land. Here during the afternoon one may see a Field-Marshal and a Cabinet Minister, an ambassador and a Duke, taking their "half-dozen" side by side. But the ordinary oyster shop makes a specialty of the Anglo-Dutch and other varieties which can be sold at a moderate rate. The arrangement of the window of the ordinary London oyster shop is of the aquarium order. Many exhibit a large specimen of the shell which we used to put to our ears as children in order to "hear the ocean roar." Some shade the window light with a brilliant green globe, others prefer a pink effect. Seaweed is occasionally used to decorate a hearthstone-coloured combination which is supposed to represent the bed of the ocean

The trade in light refreshments which is left in the hands of the kerbstone purveyor is not so great as it used to be, except perhaps in the east and south of London and certain Saturday-night thoroughfares. The oyster stalls are few and far between, and the whelk stall has of late shown a modest retirement in the west. The old lady with a basket in which trotters are laid out on a clean white cloth may still be found at certain corners, but she belongs to a rapidly disappearing body of street caterers. The trotter woman's peculiar cry is getting as rare as the muffin man's bell, and the "Fine Stor-bries" of the hawker who, basket on head, was wont, especially on Sunday afternoons, to wake the echoes of quiet streets with his trade announcement.

The cookshop which does a roaring trade in the daytime has no place here, because it supplies the solid meal of most of its customers. In the same cat-egory are the vegetarian restaurants. now liberally patronised by ladies and gentleman who abjure a flesh diet; but the foreign shops which are half in the ham and beef line and half in the tinned provision trade are doing a big light refreshment business all day long. At the counter where "Delicatessen" are purveyed you may buy and eat your sandwich, and have it made of un-English ingredients—sardines, German, French, and Italian sausage, smoked sal-mon, occasionally even of caviare. These establish-ments have generally a refreshment room upstairs, where you may have coffee, chocolate and cakes, or sweet and savoury snacks. Here you may even pur-chase the herring salad dear to the sons of the Fatherland, and eat it while you wait or take it home in a paper bag.

All these forms of light refreshment are to be found in the west. Let us wend our way east, and study the crowded menus of, say, Mile End Road.

This seems to be a neighbourhood where light

refreshment is a leading industry. Not only do the stalls on the kerbstone offer the passer-by delicacies of various descriptions, but in main thoroughfare and side street alike you find shop after shop catering for the appetite that requires "a small contribution." Here is a pastrycook's with a side room packed with young people, mostly of the Hebrew race, who are taking coffee and cakes. Here is a cookshop in which white-shirt-sleeved assistants are continually attacking "spotted dogs" and "curranty" rolls with a knife, and deftly turning the slice into a piece of paper for the hand stretched out to secure it. A favourite "dish" at these establishments is a kind of batter pudding. When you have your penny slice of this in a piece of paper the assistant pours over it a spoonful of the gravy in which the remains of a loin of pork are standing. Why the gravy does not run over on to the floor I cannot say. I only know that it does not. When the batter pudding client comes out into the street with his light refreshment in his hand and commences to eat it the gravy is there still.

The fried fish shop of the east is very like the fried fish shop of the west, but in the matter of "chips" there is a slight difference. It is in the vinegar bottle. It may be the desire of the East-Ender to get more for his money, but this I know, that where the

West-End "chipper" is contented just to sprinkle his or her pennyworth, the East-End "chipper" shakes the bottle for a good two minutes in order to get a grand result. Salt for fish or for chips or for batter pudding you take with finger and thumb from a big salt box on the counter, and you bring the salt out with you and do your seasoning in the street.

Down the little dark side streets around White-chapel and Spitalfields you will find curious little shops that deal principally in olives and gherkins in salt and water. The latter are exposed in big tubs, and are often bought and eaten without ceremony on the spot. For the Russians and Roumanian Jews there are special light refreshments provided in the shops that have their fronts ornamented with Hebrew characters. There are even small refreshment counters and little coffee shops in which the menu is entirely in Yiddish.

The larger Hebrew population is responsible for the fact that many beef and ham shops are beef shops only, or substitute the huge German sausage for the familiar ham of the Gentile establishment.

The pie shops here offer you a more varied choice than at the west. In them you can buy hot beef-steak pies and puddings, eel, kidney, meat, fruit, and mince pies. There is also in Mile End Road an establishment which is famous for miles around for its baked sheeps' hearts, and another which has a reputation for tripe and onions that extends beyond the tramway system.

The stall catering of this district is extensive and peculiar. Here in all its glory the eel-jelly trade is carried on. In great white basins you see a savoury mess. Behind the stall mother and father, sometimes assisted by son and daughter, wash up cups and spoons, and ladle out the local luxury to a continuous stream of customers. Many a time on a terribly cold night have I watched a shivering, emaciated-looking man eagerly consuming his cup of eel-jelly, and only parting with the spoon and crockery when even the tongue of a dog could not have extracted another drop from either.

The shell-fish stalls are larger and more commodious than they are in the west. Under the flaring naphtha lights are set out scores of little saucers containing whelks, cockles, and mussels "a penny a plate." Oysters at these stalls are sold at sixpence a dozen. The trade, even at that price, is not large.

Hot green peas are served in teacups at some outdoor establishments. The peculiarity of this form of light refreshment is the prodigality of the customers in the matter of vinegar and pepper, which are *à discretion* and gratis. And in the east you may also purchase peanuts fresh roasted while you wait. The hot apple fritter is now, too, a street stall luxury.

The hot fruit drink is a favourite light refreshment in the East-End, where a large number of the Hebrew immigrants have no taste for the more potent beverages of the gin palace and the tavern. Everywhere you will see little shops with windows removed and counters open to the street. These establishments may include some other business, perhaps cigars or sweets or newspapers or general items, but the trade on which they rely is the hot temperance beverage.

This business is also carried on by many stall-holders; and on bitter winter nights the proprietor has all his work to do keep the boys who have no money to spend from warming themselves gratis at the pan of burning coke on which he keeps his kettle boiling.

The baked potato can is in evidence east and west during the winter months, and a "nice floury tater" is a favourite form of light refreshment with the poor. To many a poor fellow it is the evening meal. West-End youngsters have been known to purchase a baked potato in lightness of heart and to consume it "on the premises." But as a rule they refuse the peripatetic vendor's polite offer of a dab of yellow grease which he euphemistically terms "butter."

In the East-End the baked chestnut stand has its appointed place. Many roast chestnut vendors, with a bitter knowledge of the vagaries of the English climate, wheel out on Saturday afternoons prepared for meteorological eccentricities. They divide their establishment on wheels into two distinct departments, and offer you at the same time baked chestnuts and ices.

The cry of the hokey-pokey merchant is not so familiar as it used to be. "Hokey-Pokey" was the Englishing of "ecco uno poco"—"here is a little." The London boy found that the ice done up in white paper *was* too little. He preferred his "gelata" in a glass which he could hold in his hand and lick at his leisure while leaning in an easy attitude against the Italian merchant's gaily painted barrow.

In hot weather there are two temperance drink vendors who are well known in the City and who drive a big trade during the dinner-hour. These are the man with "the yellow lemonade" in a big glass bottle, with the real lemon doing duty as a cork, and the sherbet vendor. An entirely new form of liquid refreshment for small boys has come into vogue during recent years. It is the liquor left in the preserved pineapple tin after the slices of fruit have been taken out. "A halfpenny a small glass" is the price usually charged. The man who sells sarsaparilla as a beverage has sometimes a gay and attractive vehicle fitted up for the purpose. It is gorgeously labelled in gold, and wherever it stands draws around it an admiring crowd. "Herb beer" is somewhat similarly retailed.

An article on London's Light Refreshments would not be complete without a reference to the railway station buffet large and small. For many years the pork pie and the Banbury cake were held to be the ordinary food of the travelling Englishman. Of late years great improvements have taken place in railway buffet catering. A spirit of humanity has animated the directors and they no longer look upon their passengers as human ostriches. At the railway termini of London and on the many branches of the Metropolitan and North London system you can to-day obtain light refreshment that will sustain you between meals without incapacitating you for the enjoyment of life for a fortnight. Tea and coffee may be had at most of the bars at all hours; and although the hard boiled egg and the cold sausage are still displayed for the unwary and ham is the only form of sandwich known to some caterers, many little delicacies have been introduced, and there are signs of still further improvement.

G. R. M. Devereux

The last quarter of the nineteenth century saw a great deal of change in dining etiquette, as the prevailing service style for the wealthy changed from à la Française, in which a number of dishes were laid simultaneously on the table at each of several courses, to à la Russe, a more straightforwardly sequential style, generally of nine or more courses. Additionally, the second industrial revolution ushered in new technology both in the kitchen and on the table.

G. R. M Devereux was apparently 'one of the aristocracy', and offered gender-specific advice in *Etiquette for Men* (1902) and the companion volume *Etiquette for Women*. S/he also wrote *The Marriage Guide*, *The Lover's Dictionary* and a guide to letter writing, among others. This passage is not at all typical of the rather solemn tone of the rest of the volume and was – sadly – dropped from later editions.

'The Orange', from *Etiquette for Men*

ONE OF THE GREATEST DIFFICULTIES.

There is a doubt as to which of the courses holds for the novice the greatest terrors and pitfalls, but I think dessert would be generally voted the most trying, or at any rate one of the most trying. It is very difficult to eat fruit gracefully.

To help the novice as much as possible, here are some rules for eating various kinds.

THE ORANGE.

First let me advise you to avoid embarking on an orange, unless you are an adept. It requires long experience, a colossal courage, any amount of cool self-possession, and a great skill to attack and dispose of one without harm to yourself or your neighbour.

No amount of care can prevent the juice from besprinkling your own shirt front or your neighbour's gown, be she opposite or beside you. In fact no gown, no spotless shirt front within range is safe, while there certainly seems to be in the human eye some uncanny magnetism whereby it attracts to itself the juice of this pungent fruit. Tangerines are more manageable. But if after this you feel drawn to an orange or urged by a spirit of defiance to try your fortune, here is the safest and most correct mode of attack. The issue lies between you and the fruit.

Cut the orange in two, then in four pieces, afterwards cutting the pulp from the skin, and conveying it on the fork to the mouth. It sounds simple!

FRANK SCHLOESSER
1862–1913

Frank Schloesser was a minor journalist who has left little mark on literature. He wrote two books, *The Cult of the Chafing Dish*, from which this extract is taken, and *The Greedy Book*, which was apparently badly edited and rather sketchy. Schloesser was half German, the son of a music professor, and also worked as a translator. He was a regular contributor on food to *Country Life*, among other publications, and was described as 'a practical expert who prefers simplicity and plain cooking to the exaggerations of modern cuisine'.

This extract is drawn from the thoroughly tongue-in-cheek introduction, which was widely praised for its prose and recipes. A chafing dish was a simple piece of apparatus intended for use on a tabletop and comprising of a spirit-burner, a stand, and a dish for cooking in. Various attachments were available, including a toaster and an egg coddler, which Schloesser enthusiastically recommends. It had a whiff of bachelor cookery about it all. The author married at the age of forty-seven, five years after its publication.

from *The Cult of the Chafing Dish*

> "There does not at this blessed moment
> breathe on the Earth's surface a human
> being that willna prefer eating and drinking
> to all ither pleasures o' body or soul."
> —THE ETTRICK SHEPHERD.

Every bachelor has a wife of some sort. Mine is a Chafing Dish; and I desire to sing her praises.

My better half—I love to call her Chaffinda, and to dwell upon the doubled consonant—is a nickel-plated dish on a wrought-iron stand, with a simple spirit-lamp wherewith to keep herself warm. I bought her at Harrod's Stores for twelve shillings and ninepence—and she has sisters.

It has been borne in upon me that many quite nice folk may be glad to learn something of the possibilities of Chaffinda. Whether married or single, there are moments in the life of nearly every man and woman when the need of a quick, hot, and light little meal is worth much fine gold. To such I would politely address myself.

The ordinary domestic cook is a tireless enemy of the Chafing Dish. She calls it "fiddle-faddle." Maybe. But inasmuch as it is clean, economical, speedy and rather simple, it would naturally not appeal to her peculiar sense of the culinary art.

To bachelors, male and female, in chambers, lodgings, diggings, and the like, in fact to all who "batch"; to young couples with a taste for theatres, concerts, and homely late suppers; to yachtsmen, shooting-parties, and picnickers; to inventive artists who yearn for fame in the evolution of a new entrée; to invalids, night workers, actors and stock-brokers, the Chafing Dish is a welcome friend and companion.

It has its limitations, of course, but they are few and immaterial, and its obvious advantages and conveniences far outweigh its trivial drawbacks. At the same time it must be remembered that it is a serious cooking apparatus, and by no means a mere toy.

When two or three are gathered together, and one mentions the magic word "Chafing Dish," the second invariably chimes in with "Welsh Rabbit." This is an error of taste, but excusable in the circumstances. Chafing Dishes were not created for the exclusive canonisation of Welsh Rabbits, although a deft hand may occasionally play with one in a lightsome mood. There are other and better uses. All the same, a fragrant and delicate Rabbit is not to be despised, although it must not be made conceited by too great an elevation into the realms of high cookery.

I suppose that every nation has the cooks that it deserves, and, if this be accepted as an axiom, the general degeneration of the Plain Cook of the middle classes amply accounts for the growing cult of the Chafing Dish. The British school of cookery, in its mediocre form, is monotony exemplified. Too many broths spoil the cook; and hence we derive our dull sameness of roast and boiled.

Imagination and a due sense of proportion are as necessary in cooking as in any other art—more so then in some, for Impressionism in the kitchen simply means indigestion. Digestion is the business of the human interior, indigestion that of the doctor. It is so easy to cook indigestible things that a savoury cunningly concocted of Bismuth and Pepsine would seem an almost necessary adjunct to the menu (or *Carte Dinatoire*, as the French Revolutionists called it) of the budding Chafist.

But the demon of indigestion may easily be exorcised with a little care and thought. Three great apothegms should be borne in mind. Imprimis: Never worry your food; let it cook out its own salvation. Item: Use as few highly spiced condiments as possible; and, lastly, keep to natural flavours, juices, and sauces.

Much modern depravity, for instance, I attribute to the unholy cult of Mayonnaise (or Mahonnaise, or Bayonnaise, or Magnonaise, according to different culinary authorities). At its best it is simply a saucy disguise to an innocent salmon or martial lobster, reminding the clean-palated of an old actor painted up to look young. I once knew a man who proposed to a girl at a dance-supper simply because he could not think of anything else to say, and suddenly discovered that they both hated Mayonnaise. I have no reason to suppose that they are unhappy.

Another point about having a wife in the shape of a Chafing Dish is somewhat delicate to explain. Coarsely indicated, it amounts to this. Continuous intercourse with such a delicious, handy and resourceful helpmeet tends to a certain politeness in little things, a dainty courtesy which could not be engendered by the constant companionship of a common kitchen-range. Chafing-Dish cookery bears the same relation to middle-class kitchen cookery that the delightful art of fencing does to that of the broadsword. Both are useful, but there is a world of subtle differentiation between the two. The average rough and tumble of the domestic saucepan contrasts with the deft manipulation of the miniature battery of tiny pans.

AGNES JEKYLL
1861–1937

Vegetarianism was in its infancy in the early twentieth century. For much of history the majority of the population could not afford to eat meat, so voluntarily relinquishing it was seen as the choice of cranks or the highly religious. Strict Catholics still adhered to meatless fast days (fish days), which had been the British norm before the Reformation. This started to change in the late Victorian era when it became associated with health and also with feminism.

This extract uses the French term for a religious fast day, *maigre*, but its appearance in an essay in *The Times* hints at the growth of the movement more generally. Dame Agnes Jekyll was a society hostess who had gained her damehood for her work in the First World War, coordinating hospital supplies. She later devoted her energies to women and children in legal trouble. At her death, *The Times* suggested that, had she been a man, she would have been 'a great public servant'.

'Meatless Meals',
from *Kitchen Essays*

A certain *maigre* luncheon on a sunny Friday of an early summer, now far away and long ago, was vividly impressed on the mind of one of the party of four who enjoyed it, partly because of the beauty of its setting and the stimulating interest of the talk in that brief hour of refection, but also because of the discovery that such very simple things could be so much better than the elaborate and expensive ones which often complicate the sweet uses of hospitality. The garden room of an educational institution set amongst those lovely wooded hills which dip to the sea near Dublin, a Jesuit father of great intellectual distinction and goodness, a nun with a "divine plain face," and two searchers after truth—this the scene and the party.

Never before had newly-laid eggs scrambled so deliciously with young asparagus, or pink-fleshed trout tasted so fresh in the company of tiny potatoes and crisp lettuce. A wholemeal loaf and milk scones were there, with home-made cream cheese; the first fruits of the bee-hive also, tasting of the scent of lime trees in blossom, and the last fruits of the dairy in golden butter. Woodland strawberries, harbingers of the summer, in leaf-lined baskets, gave out their fugitive aroma, and finally a brown jug of coffee freshly roasted and ground, hot and fragrant beyond all previous experience, brought its valedictory blessing to a perfect meal. How gross in comparison appeared the joints of butcher's meat, the slaughtered game and poultry of daily life, until the great reconciler, custom, should blunt afresh our susceptibilities! Since meatless days are the rule of many at certain Church seasons, and of many more at all seasons, some suggestions for making *maigre* menus more generally acceptable to all may not come amiss; for did not Mary Coleridge remind us in a pleasant volume of table talk that "Self-sacrifice is the noblest thing in the world, but to sacrifice other people, even for a noble thing, is as wrong as persecution."

Here is a breakfast or high-tea notion for a busy worker on a long winter's day, when time and thoughts race too quickly for more deliberate nourishment: A crumpet with lots of butter and salt; on it an egg, or maybe two, perfectly fried, the peppermill just going out of action, and all served piping hot in a warmed muffin dish. This is moderate in cost, simple in preparation, nourishing, and nice.

Here are two soups of proved excellence—one for coast dwellers or those near a good fish-market, and owning a well-filled purse; the other for everyman and everywhere. For a restrained and anglicized *Bouillabaisse* for four—

> Make about a quart of fish stock in the usual way, with the trimmings, bones, and shell of the fish and lobster to be used subsequently. Cut up 2 large onions, and fry them in ½ gill of Lucca oil, add a teaspoonful of flour, a tumbler of white wine, pepper, salt, a fagot of parsley, a bay leaf, and 3 tablespoonfuls of tomato sauce. Boil from 15 to 20 minutes, pass through sieve, and return to saucepan. Cut up a small lobster into pieces, also a gurnet, bream, or flounder, of which the trimmings have been already utilized, for the fish stock. Boil ½ hour on a quick fire with the prepared stock, put a slice of bread, or preferably several small slices from a French roll, into a warmed tureen, transfer the fish with a strainer on to the bread, pour the broth over all, and serve together. When time is a consideration, as before some evening performance, this portmanteau of two courses is useful.

Everyman Soup, for four persons.

> Melt in a stewpan 1½ oz. butter, stir into it smoothly 2 tablespoonfuls *crême de riz* flour. Add I quart milk (or if permissible, some light veal

stock and milk mixed); let it cook for 10 minutes. Then add 2 tablespoonfuls freshly-grated parmesan or other cheese, and some pieces of macaroni previously washed and boiled in milk and cut into ¼-inch sections; or get some of those small shell-shaped Italian pastes called *coquilli* procurable fresh in Soho. Just before serving, pour the boiling soup on to a yolk of egg mixed with a little cream; stir all smooth, and pour into a hot marmite pot.

Clever *maigre* combinations of eggs, fish, vegetables, and fruit give abundant scope for culinary talent. Try for a useful luncheon dish:—

Œufs Mollels. Sauce Fromage.
Boil your finest eggs soft inside, firm when peeled and skinned; balance them on circlets of fried bread within a low rampart of dry boiled rice; send them round with a bowl of bubbling hot cheese sauce made by stirring into a pint of nicest thin béchamel a ¼ lb. grated cheddar; to be ladled out over the eggs and rice.

If your cook has the puff-pastry touch, a *Vol-au-Vent* case confers distinction on all manner of noble relics, united in the bonds of a good sauce. Sea-kale boiled tender in milk and cut into short lengths, and diluted with béchamel, varieties of haricot beans, mildly curried and mixed with cauliflower, remains of fish with lobster or shrimp sauce, and, best of all, creamed oysters, will compose suitable fillings if skilfully treated.

Thatched House Pudding.

This old country-house favourite is really too nice for Lenten fare, but it could give opportunities for self-denial, and might come in usefully at any season. It is worth rehearsing into perfection if the first attempt should prove a little uncertain. Melt 2 oz. butter, add 4 tablespoonfuls flour. Pour in enough boiling milk to the consistence of a hasty pudding; add yolks of 4 eggs and grated rind of 1 lemon, with a little juice and sugar to taste. Whisk the whites stiffly, and add to the mixture. Put all in an oven-proof dish (a Pyrex glass one, 10½ inches by 6½ inches by 2 inches, just holds this quantity for six or seven). Cook from 15 to 20 minutes. Before serving and after it has risen, pour over the top a cupful of hot thin apricot jam, and sprinkle with a liberal ounce of browned and chopped almonds.

With so many good things for meatless menus to choose from, our thoughts need never turn to what we lack, but rather find contentment in all we have.

Countess Morphy
1883–1938

Marcelle Azra Hincks was not a countess, nor was she called Morphy, but it was under that pseudonym that she wrote a series of books about dancing and, later, cookery. She wrote warmly and well, and also gave cookery classes at Selfridges.

One of the loveliest books of the 1930s, her *Recipes of All Nations* is indicative of a growing interest in global foods apparent between the wars. French food remained the cuisine to aspire to, but American tastes in particular were making headway in Britain (mainly in the form of terrible salads). This book goes still further, with sections on most European countries, plus China, Japan, India, the US, Hincks' natal town of New Orleans and 'many lands'. For those sections not drawn from her own experience, she consulted others, mainly London-based restaurateurs. This recipe, however, was contributed by a Mr Moritz, a 'gourmet with an unbiased mind'.

'Fricassée of Iguana',
from *Recipes of All Nations*

Fricassée of Iguana is another favourite dish in Guinea. The iguana is a large, edible lizard which is prepared in various ways—roasted, grilled, or in the oven. At certain times of the year, when the females are full of eggs, it is much esteemed, as the eggs are considered a great delicacy. The back only of the animal is used for this fricassée, which is delicious. The pieces of iguana are cooked in hot butter in a casserole and, when browned, a little flour is sprinkled over them. When the whole is browned, a little water is added, as well as parsley, bayleaf and thyme, and a few small onions. This is simmered for about ¾ of an hour, the eggs being added only a few minutes before serving.

FRANCIS LADRY
1889–1966
'Lord Woolton Pie'

Lord Woolton Pie is one of the iconic recipes of the Second World War. It was invented by Francis Ladry, chef at the Savoy, as part of a series of public campaigns to maintain morale in the face of stringent food rationing. Lord Woolton (Frederick Marquis, first earl of Woolton) was head of the Ministry of Food, to which he'd been appointed due to his background as a successful businessman and social economist. Politically neutral, he was a crucial part of the wartime government, and it was largely due to his efforts that rationing was accepted for so long by the British public.

Rationing was introduced on 8 January 1940 and was not finally lifted until 4 July 1954. The health of the nation improved through a guaranteed (limited) meat supply, and a diet high in fruit and vegetables but low in fats and sugar. It was unutterably monotonous, however, and this recipe is no exception.

'Lord Woolton Pie'

The Times, 26 April 1941

LORD WOOLTON PIE
THE OFFICIAL RECIPE

In hotels and restaurants, no less than in communal canteens, many people have tasted Lord Woolton pie and pronounced it good. Like many another economical dish, it can be described as wholesome fare. It also meets the dietician's requirements in certain vitamins. The ingredients can be varied according to the vegetables in season. Here is the official recipe:—

Take 1lb each diced of potatoes, cauliflower, swedes, and carrots, three or four spring onions—if possible, one teaspoonful of vegetable extract, and one tablespoonful of oatmeal. Cook all together for 10 minutes with just enough water to cover. Stir occasionally to prevent the mixture from sticking. Allow to cool; put into a piedish, sprinkle with chopped parsley, and cover with a crust of potato or wheatmeal pastry. Bake in a moderate oven until the pastry is nicely browned and serve hot with a brown gravy.

❦

GEORGE ORWELL
1903–1950

One of the most renowned British writers of the twentieth century, George Orwell (Eric Blair) is best known for his post-war satires, *Animal Farm* and *1984*. His other books frequently drew on his own experiences, including a stint living rough, but he was also a skilled polemicist. This article appeared in the *Evening Standard* in December 1945, and led to a commission from the British Council to write a longer version, intended to encourage tourists. It was not published, the Council deciding that extolling the delights of food when most of post-war Europe didn't have any was a tad insensitive.

Orwell's list of British delicacies looks back to the 1930s. Many of the foods he lusts after were no longer available in a time of rationing, and many, indeed, never really came back. The small-scale cheese industry, in particular, was virtually wiped out by wartime regulation.

'In Defence of English Cooking'

We have heard a good deal of talk in recent years about the desirability of attracting foreign tourists to this country. It is well known that England's two worst faults, from a foreign visitor's point of view, are the gloom of our Sundays and the difficulty of buying a drink.

Both of these are due to fanatical minorities who will need a lot of quelling, including extensive legislation. But there is one point on which public opinion could bring about a rapid change for the better: I mean cooking.

It is commonly said, even by the English themselves, that English cooking is the worst in the world. It is supposed to be not merely incompetent, but also imitative, and I even read quite recently, in a book by a French writer, the remark: "The best English cooking is, of course, simply French cooking".

Now that is simply not true. As anyone who has lived long abroad will know, there is a whole host of delicacies which it is quite impossible to obtain outside the English-speaking countries. No doubt the list could be added to, but here are some of the things that I myself have sought for in foreign countries and failed to find.

First of all, kippers, Yorkshire pudding, Devonshire cream, muffins and crumpets. Then a list of puddings that would be interminable if I gave it in full: I will pick out for special mention Christmas pudding, treacle tart and apple dumplings. Then an almost equally long list of cakes: for instance, dark plum cake (such as you used to get at Buzzard's before the war), short-bread and saffron buns. Also innumerable kinds of biscuit, which exist, of course, elsewhere, but are generally admitted to be better and crisper in England.

Then there are the various ways of cooking potatoes that are peculiar to our own country. Where else do you see potatoes roasted under the joint, which is far and away the best way of cooking them? Or the delicious potato cakes that you get in the north of England? And it is far better to cook new potatoes in the English way—that is, boiled with mint and then served with a little melted butter or margarine—than to fry them as is done in most countries.

Then there are the various sauces peculiar to England. For instance, bread sauce, horse-radish sauce, mint sauce and apple sauce; not to mention redcurrant jelly, which is excellent with mutton as well as with hare, and various kinds of sweet pickle, which we seem to have in greater profusion than most countries.

What else? Outside these islands I have never seen a haggis, except one that came out of a tin, nor Dublin prawns, nor Oxford marmalade, nor several other kinds of jam (marrow jam and bramble jelly, for instance), nor sausages of quite the same kind as ours.

Then there are the English cheeses. There are not many of them but I fancy that Stilton is the best cheese of its type in the world, with Wensleydale not far behind. English apples are also outstandingly good, particularly the Cox's Orange Pippin.

And finally, I would like to put in a word for English bread. All the bread is good, from the enormous Jewish loaves flavoured with caraway seeds to the Russian rye bread which is the colour of black treacle. Still, if there is anything quite as good as the soft part of the crust from an English cottage loaf (how soon shall we be seeing cottage loaves again?) I do not know of it.

No doubt some of the things I have named above could be obtained in continental Europe, just as it is possible in London to obtain vodka or bird's nest soup. But they are all native to our shores, and over huge areas they are literally unheard of.

South of, say, Brussels, I do not imagine that you

would succeed in getting hold of a suet pudding. In French there is not even a word that exactly translates "suet". The French, also, never use mint in cookery and do not use blackcurrants except as a basis of a drink.

It will be seen that we have no cause to be ashamed of our cookery, so far as originality goes or so far as the ingredients go. And yet it must be admitted that there is a serious snag from the foreign visitor's point of view. This is, that you practically don't find good English cooking outside a private house. If you want, say, a good, rich slice of Yorkshire pudding you are more likely to get it in the poorest English home than in a restaurant, which is where the visitor necessarily eats most of his meals.

It is a fact that restaurants which are distinctively English and which also sell good food are very hard to find. Pubs, as a rule, sell no food at all, other than potato crisps and tasteless sandwiches. The expensive restaurants and hotels almost all imitate French cookery and write their menus in French, while if you want a good cheap meal you gravitate naturally towards a Greek, Italian or Chinese restaurant. We are not likely to succeed in attracting tourists while England is thought of as a country of bad food and unintelligible by-laws. At present one cannot do much about it, but sooner or later rationing will come to an end, and then will be the moment for our national cookery to revive. It is not a law of nature that every restaurant in England should be either foreign or bad, and the first step towards an improvement will be a less long-suffering attitude in the British public itself.

Evening Standard, 15 December 1945.

NEVIL SHUTE
1899–1960

Post-war Britain was a gloomy, ragged place. Food rationing got worse, and for the first time included bread. Nevil Shute Norway (he dropped his surname for writing) emigrated to Australia. An aeronautical engineer turned popular author, Nevil Shute is best known for *On the Beach* and *A Town Like Alice*. His novels blend romance with adventure, with sympathetically drawn characters, both men and women, mostly in wartime or contemporary settings. Shute left Britain because he felt it had lost its independent spirit, and was a broken country.

In *The Far Country*, Shute sets Britain and Australia up as lands of contrast, the one a place of opportunity, the other where an old lady may starve to death. In truth, rationing never got quite that bad, but its impact was long-lasting and deep. It lasted sufficiently long that a whole generation grew up with only the vaguest knowledge of the possibilities of pre-war cuisine, amidst a depleted culinary landscape.

It would take another thirty years before the start

238

of a renaissance in British cuisine, and another generation would pass before British food truly regained its identity. But that is another story, a different dinner, perhaps, and for a different day.

from *The Far Country*

Jack Dorman went out to the yard, and Jane began to lay the kitchen table for the midday dinner. She was vaguely unhappy and uneasy; there was a menace in all the news from England now, both in the letters from her old aunt and in the newspapers. The most extraordinary things seemed to be going on there, and for no reason at all. In all her life, and it had been a hard life at times, she had never been short of all the meat that she could eat, or practically any other sort of food or fruit that she desired. As a child she could remember the great joints upon her father's table at Sutton Bassett, the kidneys and bacon for breakfast with the cold ham on the sideboard, the thick cream on the table, the unlimited butter. These things were as normal to her as the sun or the wind; even in the most anxious times of their early married life in Gippsland they had had those things as a matter of course, and never thought about them. If she didn't use them now so much it was because she was older and felt better on a sparing diet, but it was almost inconceivable to her that they should not be there for those who wanted them.

It was the same with coal; in all her life she had never had to think about economizing with fuel.

From the blazing fireplaces and kitchen range of Sutton Bassett she had gone to the Australian countryside, milder in climate, where everybody cooked and warmed themselves with wood fires. Even in their hardest times there had never been any question of unlimited wood for fuel. Indeed, at Merrijig with the hot sun and the high rainfall the difficulty was to keep the forest from encroaching on the paddocks; if you left a corner ungrazed for three years the bush would be five feet high all over it; in ten it would have merged back into forest. Even in the city you ordered a ton of wood as naturally as a pound of butter or a sirloin of beef.

Whatever sort of way could Aunt Ethel be living in when she could not afford a warm vest for the winter? Why *a* warm vest – why not three or four? She must do something about the washing. Was clothing rationed still? She seemed to remember that clothes rationing had been removed in England. She stopped laying the table and unfolded the letter and read the passage over again, a little frown of perplexity upon her forehead. There wasn't anything about rationing; she hadn't got the vest because it was expensive. How foolish of her; old people had to have warm clothes, especially in England in the winter. It was true that the price of woollen garments was going up even in Australia by leaps and bounds, but Aunt Ethel couldn't possibly be as hard up as that. The Foxleys had always had plenty of money. Perhaps she was going a bit senile.

She went and rang the dinner bell outside the flyscreen door, rather depressed.

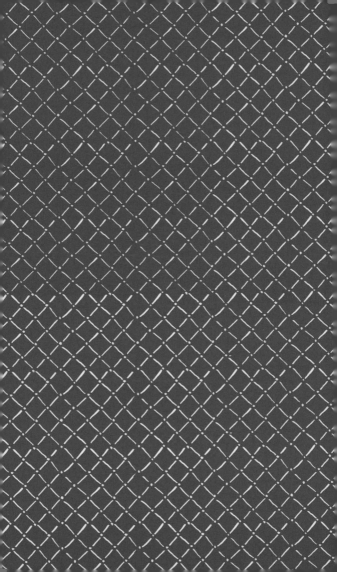